WHEN DREAMS DON'T WORK
Professional Caregivers and Burnout

Ronna F. Jevne
and
Donna Reilly Williams

Death, Value and Meaning Series
Series Editor: John D. Morgan

Baywood Publishing Company, Inc.
AMITYVILLE, NEW YORK

Library of Congress Catalog Number: 97-28442
ISBN: 0-89503-179-5 (hardcover)

Library of Congress Cataloging-in-Publication Data

Jevne, Ronna Fay.
    When dreams don't work : professional caregivers and burnout /
Ronna F. Jevne and Donna Reilly Williams.
      p.   cm. - - (Death, value and meaning series)
  Includes bibliographic references and index.
  ISBN 0-89503-179-5 (hardcover)
    1. Burn out (Psychology)   2. Work- -Psychological aspects.
I. Williams, Donna Reilly, 1945- . II. Title. III. Series
BF481.J48   1998
158.7'23- -dc21   97-28442
                                         CIP

Dedication

We dedicate this book to our husbands, Allen and Cliff, who have believed in and supported our dreams.

Acknowledgments

We acknowledge the contributions of the many whose dreams have been broken and revisioned. We are grateful to Karen Stocker, who drew the figures for the grief diagrams, Mike Bell, who opened up to us the world of Organizational Vision and Bobbi Olszewski at Baywood Publishing Company, whose patience and encouragement have greatly facilitated the completion of this book. As co-authors we want to celebrate our writing journey as one of mutual respect, open communication, and collaborative spirit.

Table of Contents

CHAPTER 9

Introduction

Are you a professional caregiver? Does your work rely on your being able to reach out, able to privilege your client, student, or patient's needs over your own? Are you, for some reason, unable to live out your dream of what it means to be a professional? Have the recent economic changes and the directing of resources away from human services affected your life? Are you caught in the jaws of managed care or agencies which seem to have a very different vision from your own? Do you sometimes wonder if there is any point in caring? Is your vision of life's potential changing without your consent?

We, the authors (Ronna and Donna), are people of passion. Throughout our professional lives, we have ventured into many institutional settings, from pre-school to graduate school, through hospitals, hospices, and into local parish ministry. In all those environments, we have met colleagues whose professional journeys have lost their excitement and energy. Involvement in training programs for caring professionals has shown us that very little energy is spent on preparing future caregivers to avoid the disillusioning and heartbreaking experience we call *burnout*. Based on these observations and on our passion for *something better*, we have chosen to write a book for caregivers who are experiencing the loss of their dreams, for students who are just beginning to articulate theirs, and for educators who hope to encourage their students to be as holistic and life competent about their unfolding professional journeys as possible.

1

We wanted to write a book which would offer hope. Hope is intimately interwoven and embedded in our dreams—our personal dreams and our professional dreams. No one begins life saying, "When I grow up, I want to be divorced, ill, and unhappily employed." We formulate life dreams, imagined maps for where we hope life will take us—or we will take life—full of excitement and hope. When our dreams do not come true, we are painfully disillusioned.

When Dreams Don't Work is an opportunity for you as a professional caregiver to reflect upon your life journey and come to discern and embrace your own hopes and dreams. This is not a book that lays out a simple program to avoid or heal from burnout. In fact, some of what it contains will likely challenge its readers in very difficult ways. The questions it will invite you to address about your own life dreams and attitudes may challenge your present views about the world of work and the ways you fit into that world.

For those who train future caregivers, we offer suggestions for self-reflection which might assist in "vaccinating" your students against burnout. You see them come into your classrooms brimming with idealism and excitement. A few years later they return, already disappointed and frustrated, because somehow their caregiver dreams are not working in their own lives or in the existing institutional structures. You may have even asked yourself, "How do I prepare them for what really exists? How can I support them, helping them to keep their humanity and escape burnout?"

Borrowed dreams seldom work. Our thesis in this book is that *the degree to which each person examines and makes authentic his or her own vision, letting go of whatever is borrowed or inherited from others, is the degree to which he or she will be able to sustain a career as a professional caregiver in the contemporary environment.*

Like many of the most worthwhile quests in life, the quest for authenticity outlined in this book may lead you through deep forests and over high mountains. You may experience burning pain and frozen loneliness along the way. We hope you will have *ah-ha's* that delight you, memories that nourish you, and reflections that invite you to laughter and joy. In the end, we hope you will feel you have a roadmap to an authentic life dream and your heart and soul will know integration and peace.

Our interest was stimulated by a study of hundreds of teachers who left their classrooms due to illness. For three years, a team from the Educational Psychology Department of the University of Alberta in Canada [1] invited these people to share their experiences, their pain, and their healing journeys. Startled by the fact that once-impassioned teachers were at risk for illness, the study led to an understanding of the importance of the professional dream in the lives of those who choose career pathways that involve a vision of helping others.

The teachers shared their journeys from dedication to debilitation. What they shared was surprisingly different from what the research teams anticipated. When professionals from other helping disciplines read the report, the head nodding was always accompanied with, "This is not just about teachers. This is scary; I can see myself in this."

The expected relationships between lifestyle, coping style, and skills was not forthcoming as a distinguishing feature of the study. The surprising component was the loss of the professional dream.

The last decade in North America has seen growth in the mind/body movement, which emphasizes integration of emotional and physical self-care. Professional caregivers are beginning to realize that the human experience cannot be dichotomized; there are strong connections between the human psyche and physical health.

Even before the Alberta Teachers' Study, we as caregivers were coming to understand the strong connection between stress and disease. However, because we have not understood the importance of the professional dream to caregiver wellness, we have centered prevention and treatment programs on the symptoms, not the underlying causes of the problem. These programs encourage people to do things differently—or properly—to acquire more skills—yoga, diet, exercise, and time planning. The assumption is simply that, by doing all these things more competently, one will not burn out or become ill.

These programs ignore the fact that for some people, just the task of *doing* all these things is stressful! How many of us have grasped for hope through such a program, only to find that we have bodies that can't do jogging, a mind which does not respond to the disciplines of yoga, or a life which simply does not accommodate to these strategies? Then, where is our hope? What is offered to those of us whose lifestyles simply will not allow those changes? Are there any alternative choices for people who would actually be stressed by these life changes?

Do you resonate with the above paragraph? We both love it! It fits who we are—ordinary people who believe in healthy living, but who also enjoy relaxation, rich food, play, and lots and lots of really hard work, often with erratic schedules. Are we doomed to burnout while our more disciplined colleagues will enjoy health?

In fact, through the Alberta study, we learned that what many people had suspected was true. Even many of those who made all the lifestyle changes became ill.

Positive lifestyle changes, especially exercise, diet, and the cessation of substance abuse, are certainly important to overall health. They are not, however, the deciding factors in the disillusionment, agony, and physical breakdown of burnout.

In a delightful book *One Hundred over 100: Moments with One Hundred North American Centenarians,* 100 centenarians shared their views on life [2]. They had all said, "Yes!" to life for over one hundred years! Many of us will be pleased to hear that these people are not necessarily non-smoking vegetarians who have been happily married to one person for eighty years. One fellow did say that had he realized how long he was going to live, he would have taken better care of himself. There are those who were pioneer health nuts and those who have been addicted to alcohol for eight decades. Some have recovered from cancer three times; some have undone their I *do*'s four times! What these people have in common is a quiet *gusto*—a non-aggressive determination, a soft fortitude, a relentless involvement with life. They love life and they have passionate interests—music, work, sports, children, and literature—always accompanied with a concern for those beyond themselves.

Over those one hundred years, they witnessed amazing changes. They were at times disabled, disenfranchised, and discouraged. They survived the 1918 Spanish Influenza epidemic, which claimed forty million lives, and lived through two world wars. They were neither embarrassed to love nor ashamed to be tough.

Through all these trials, in all life's tests, their personal dreams sometimes needed to be reexamined and revalued. They did not, however, lose sight of who they were. Their personhood was more vital than any crisis or experience. They could cope as long as they had a sense of vision which allowed them to hope. This same reality is described by survivors of Nazi concentration camps [3]. In that environment, staying mentally stable demanded that one understand the core meaning of who one was—and who one was not.

The sense of who one is, and of one's empowering life vision, seems to be at the core of long and creative living. If a person builds her vision based on something less authentic, then she is like the man in Matthew's Gospel [4] who built his house on the sand. There is nothing secure on which that vision is anchored and the storms of life can wash it away. Up to now, treatment regimes have paid attention to the hurts of the house breaking up and being washed out to sea.

Teachers in the Alberta study pointed to the need for a person's life vision to be strongly and securely built on the rock-hard base of authentic life dreams and appropriate systems to support those dreams.

In sharing this project with other people, we became aware that there are two experiences which people call *burnout*. The first is described in the statement, "Jack is completely burned out. He's been working night and day on that project. He needs to take a vacation before he begins something new." This sentence describes fatigue or exhaustion.

What we are calling *burnout* is something much deeper. While fatigue is a symptom, burnout itself is experienced in the body, the intellect, and the spirit. It is a profound sense of loss of, separation from oneself. It permeates every aspect of life and relationships, both personal and professional. It is the death of and grieving for one's life dream.

Just as we have been trained to separate mind and body in treatment of illness, we have also been encouraged to separate personal from professional life. "Leave your personal problems at home when you come to work!" was the advice we gave and were given. Losing touch with our selfhood and immersing ourselves into our professional identities is a major step along the Burnout Path. *"I am a teacher." "I am a nurse."* Until we can identify our "selves" aside from our professions, we are unable to recognize and embrace our own authentic life dreams. When we come to know ourselves as separate from our identities as people who care for the needs of others, we can discover our own unique vocations.

Hayward has taught sixth grade for eleven years. He is married and has a son and a daughter. He came to the counselor's office saying, "I have everything I ever thought I wanted. I'm a really good teacher. I love my wife and kids. I don't understand why every Sunday evening, I have a headache. I dread going back to work the next day. What's happening to me?"

Through therapy, Hayward gradually came to understand that he was a teacher not because he wanted to be, but because as a young man, he had rebelled against the elitist attitude of his parents, and chosen a profession which they thought was "lowly." Instead of rejoicing at his own gifts for working with young people, he had always accepted the "failure" definition of his parents. He began to search for a more authentic way to live out his gifts. He returned to graduate school and is studying to become a family therapist, becoming more and more excited with each class he takes. He hopes that in the end, he can take the new skills he is learning into the school system as a school counselor.

Janice has been a nurse for ten years. She is single and has risen to a position of influence in a large teaching hospital. But she is frustrated daily because with healthcare cutbacks, she cannot practice the profession she loves in ways she believes it should be done. Lately, she has been experiencing gastrointestinal upsets every Wednesday when the hospital holds management meetings. These problems last through the next couple of days as she carries out the mandates of her superiors and ensures that those in her supervision also carry them out.

Last week, Janice went to an internist because of her GI problems. The doctor could not find any reason for her difficulties, and therefore suggested that life stress might be making her ill. Now Janice is faced with acknowledging how frustrated and disappointed she is, and with trying to solve the problem of working in a system which does not sustain her professional vision.

As authors and therapists, we are aware that no experience is universal. Some of what we write may not fit your own experience. If you are a student reading this or someone who wants to use the insights of the book to support others, you may not personally resonate with some sections of this book. It is important to keep in mind that we are writing about general trends. We are analyzing general processes from the experiences of those with whom we have come in contact through our own lives. Nothing fits for everyone. We do, however, believe that what we have written here will be significant to the majority of at-risk people, and that paying attention to these insights will be useful to other professionals in assessing risk and planning healing both for themselves and for those for whom they care.

It may also be helpful to be aware, as you read, that there is no intended judgment in our descriptions of what we believe is the burnout process. We believe that most parents have done their very best to bring up healthy, well-adjusted children; that it is normal, not a sign of weakness, to learn negative self-messages from others, and that people whose dreams are inauthentic or who have invested those dreams in unreceptive systems are neither weak nor foolish. We believe that life is difficult and sometimes support from others can help when maneuvering through the journey of life. In this spirit, we offer our thoughts, reflections, and insights.

Visioning and revisioning takes time and thought. At the end of each chapter, to assist you with the journey, is a list of questions for reflection. You might want to choose a reflection partner. It's always nice to have a companion on the journey. You will want to choose this partner carefully. Look for someone who will respect your ability to discern your own life dreams, and who will not try to pull you into her dreams. Buying into other people's dreams is what this book tries to prevent or change. Be sure you both understand that the reason for the partnership is to validate each other's unique visions. Do your writing and reflecting separately, and then come together to share what you have written.

The other way to do the reflections is to allow yourself time and quiet space to reflect upon each question. Writing your reflections helps you remain centered. Read the book slowly and immerse yourself in the journey. After you have completed each set of reflections, write a sentence that begins with, "Through this set of reflections, I have learned _____."

If, through reading the book and doing the reflections, you have decided to make some life changes, then go ahead. It may be very helpful to find a support person—perhaps a counselor or spiritual director—to guide you on the quest for your own dream. Step gently, respecting yourself and others whose lives may be impacted by your changes.

Spend some time now with the following questions. If you are working with another person, remember that you are not called upon to question each other's answers, but to listen and validate each other's search. If you are working alone, pamper yourself by creating a space which is private, comfortable, and honors your quest.

1. Why are you reading this book? (Remember—there are no right or wrong answers.)
2. What have been your assumptions about people who burn out? What symptoms do you describe as burnout-related?
3. What factors have you believed are at the core of who burns out and who doesn't?

REFERENCES

1. R. F. J. Jevne and H. W. Zingle, *Striving for Health: Living with Broken Dreams,* Alberta School Employee Benefit Plan and University of Alberta, Edmonton, 1992.
2. J. Haynen, photographs by Paul Boyer, *One Hundred over 100: Moments with One Hundred North American Centenarians,* Western Producer Prairie Books, Saskatoon, Saskatchewan, 1990.
3. V. E. Frankl, *Man's Search for Meaning: An Introduction to Logotherapy,* Washington Square Press, Inc. New York, 1959 and Beacon Press, Boston, 4th Edition, 1992.
4. Matthew 7:24-27.

CHAPTER 1

Dreaming

. . . your young men shall see visions,
your old men shall dream dreams.
Acts 2:17

I have a dream!
Martin Luther King, Jr.

Tony came from an immigrant family that moved to the United States after World War II. The ethic in this family was to overcome what they had lost, through hard work and honest relationships. All seven children graduated from university near the top of their classes and continued through life creating brilliant careers. Tony went to medical school and became a surgeon.

Tony's dream had many factors which he believed could sustain him. First of all, he wanted his children never to experience poverty. Second, he wanted to help other people, and third, he wanted to be his own boss. Tony had a deep need to prove that he was "as good as" anyone.

By itself, there is no problem with any of these dream components; together, they are a recipe for burnout.

Through the years, Tony developed a healthy practice which kept his family (wife and three children) in a very comfortable lifestyle. But as his youngest child reached the age of seventeen and decided that she wanted to be an artist, Tony's dream was ripped apart. He had worked so hard for all these years, and now his daughter was choosing a profession which could mean she would experience the poverty he had been trying to prevent.

About that same time, insurance companies began to flex their muscles, telling Tony which procedures he could perform and when. His judgments about the needs of his patients became secondary to the judgments of some faceless voice on the telephone who only looked at the patients as statistics on pieces of paper. At the same time, the hospitals at which he practiced were tightening up financially, asking physicians to justify more and more costs.

Tony's autonomy, sometimes his ability to help his patients, and his professional credibility were challenged. His family was beginning to reject his value system. As more and more tension erupted in the home, Tony stayed away and dedicated more time to his practice—encountering more frustration at work.

Will Tony burn out? On what basis do you think he will or will not? If he does, who or what will have been responsible? Do you see coping skills in Tony which may prevent burnout? If you see warning signs, how capable do you think Tony is of changing? In what ways would he need to change? Read on to discover the accuracy of your prognosis.

DREAMS AND SOCIETY

If society were a ship on which we all lived and related, this ship would be afloat on an ocean of dreams. Dreams support and enliven all human interaction. The history of humanity is the history of dreams and dream makers. Often, dream makers become society's leaders, the captains of the dream ships. The rest of the people sail through life on the visions of those few.

The mark of a dream maker is the willingness not only to have a dream, but to commit to it. Some dream makers commit alone while the rest of the world disagrees. Others inspire multitudes of followers with their dreams.

In ancient times, Moses experienced his God, and invested, and then spoke his dream so strongly that he was able to lead his people for forty years through desert and wars, to the culmination of that dream. His dream became the dream of many. Moses never experienced his *Land of Milk and Honey*, but today the nation of Israel is based firmly upon his dream, and many are still willing to offer their lives to preserve what they think that dream should mean.

The "American Dream" of the United States is invested in the ideals of independence, equality, and prosperity. The core of this dream is the myth that *any American could become president.* Its symbols are many, especially a huge statue standing in the ocean holding a torch representing the dream. That statue, the gift of a European nation, showed the world that the vision of freedom and justice inherent in the American dream had extended to Europe. And in 1989, a model of that statue served as a symbol of the liberation struggle of the Chinese students in Tienanmen Square.

Dreams which have inspired many followers have not always been based on such noble ideals. Domination dreams also have obviously had appeal throughout history.

Hitler had a dream for Nazi Germany, bearing his ideal of a master race, conquering the world. He believed that if he could just put enough soldiers and war machines behind his dream, it would come true. And he went a long way toward making it happen! Today when we examine the ideals of Hitler's dream, to many it seems incredible that so many were willing to support him. But even today, on almost every continent, there are groups of people who espouse Nazi ideals and work to bring about their realization in society. Similarly, hundreds of people were willing to sacrifice their own lives and those of their children for the dream which built a village called Jonestown. Others were prepared to die in Waco, Texas, as the world watched in horror. These realities are testimony to the toxic power of some dreams.

There have always been those few people who dream broadly, creating visions in which many others can invest. We call these broad visions *corporate dreams.* All institutions and countries have corporate dreams. Not surprisingly, most of our personal dreams have major components of several corporate dreams— the dreams of the societies in which we live, the companies who employ us, the religions in which we invest our faith lives, and other community groups to which we belong. Even our own families may have a corporate dream. Certainly, that was the case with Tony's family, as outlined at the beginning of this chapter. Part of Tony's stress arose from the fact that some members of his family were attempting to diversify the dream.

Religious groups are all based on corporate dreams. The messages in the Gospels and the Koran and the holy books of each religious group are the articulation of dreams for a world of respect and holiness and each of these dreams arose from the hearts of a few individuals.

Since their inception, the corporate dreams of religious groups have often been the basis for the dreams of nations. Much of the United States was settled by people of faith from other countries, who came to a new land just so they could find the freedom to live their lives according to their religions. Others came because they were seeking more followers for their religious dreams.

Observing the dissension among seemingly homogeneous groups—for example, Christian churches—it is clear that a corporate dream, while inspiring many, may also be open to many interpretations. It is important to understand this reality because it means that achieving individual health may not necessarily mean leaving a system supported by a corporate dream, but rather learning a different personal interpretation of the same dream.

Corporate dreams, if they have enough inspiring power, may spread from one institution to another. To think only intellectually and not emotionally may be an impossible task. To separate spiritual values from social values creates fragmentation of the individual. In the United States, in spite of the ideal of separation of church and state, the ongoing "political" debate over "family values" as interpreted by differing faith groups through their religious dreams, has floated or sunk many politicians and consumed a great deal of both the economic and the creative judicial resources. While many tire of this debate, we also realize that it is vitally important that it can happen freely. When a corporate dream becomes rigid, the group espousing it becomes endangered. Experiences such as Jonestown and Waco show the toxicity of a dream that will not allow individual interpretation.

It is impossible to live in our world without investing, to some extent, in one or more of the larger dreams. Even the hippies of the 1960s, who withdrew from what they thought was the unhealthy dream of their parents' generation, were following a pattern of rebellion and reinvestment. Like the first settlers in the United States, they were withdrawing from established societies to live their dream of peace and love. While their dream may have been voiced more as political issues and less as religious values, the components of the dream and the withdrawal from existing systems were similar to so many before them. Their foreparents in the United States, the Afrikaaners in South Africa, and many other groups have formed new societies based on active rejection of the corporate dreams of the societies in which they lived.

Other institutions serve the function of reinforcing sanctioned dreams. Our educational systems are designed to guide and instill the corporate dreams of society. There may be more than one system operating concurrently, but even when this happens, there is common ground. In the United States, for example, where various school systems have developed to protect the dreams of different groups, every school day and parent meeting begins with a salute to the flag of the country, which also flies in front of every school—the symbol of the larger corporate dream.

Dreams which last through time and which unfailingly attract followers are invariably those with flexibility for individual interpretation. This room for interpretation is vital because within any large corporate dream are many, many individual dreams. Just as each person invests in one or many corporate dreams, so each of us, as we are growing up, builds a dream for our own lives. Like corporate dreams, some of these individual dreams are healthy and work very well, while others are doomed to fail. Unfortunately, discovering which dreams will work is not easy and this is often only accomplished in hindsight, after the dream has crashed, taking the individual's psyche, spirit, and sometimes physical health down with it. This crash is the phenomenon we call *burnout*.

BURNOUT AND BROKEN DREAMS

The term *burnout* is only a few years old. The phenomenon is a function of societal evolution. When we began to notice the psychological and physical breakdown of large groups of people, we began to look for a cause. When we noticed that these people were largely concentrated in a handful of professions, we assumed that the cause of burnout likely lay within those work environments and the kinds of people who chose them.

As with most newly-discovered phenomena, since scientific research was not available, we began to guess at answers based on what we observed combined with earlier insights about similar situations and our own best instincts. In the past twenty years, we have developed some very in-depth theories about stress and burnout.

What do you think are the characteristics of people who burn out? Are they factors of personality? Who is the prime candidate? Is it the "workaholic" who finally crashes—the person who never golfs, who works weekends, and never leaves for vacation without a book? Is it the incompetent worker, the weak link in the chain of productivity or success? What role do you think education plays in preventing professional exhaustion? What role does the work environment play? Let us explore the direction of new research on burnout.

The old view was that our attention must be on the individual. Certain people were thought to be more vulnerable to stress by virtue of their work habits, their personality traits, and their competence. Surely, we thought, long hours, too much responsibility, a lack of control, and inadequate training could combine with certain personality traits and personal backgrounds as a recipe for fallout from a profession.

New information, however, is being generated by studies like the teachers' study of which we have spoken. This new information disputes many of the commonly-held myths. The teachers' study found that although these myths are solidly entrenched in our thinking, the reality is that illness is not solely or specifically associated with disliking the profession, with poor coping styles, with training or competence, or with lifestyle issues. Indeed, one of the characteristics of teachers who became ill was their belief that, "It won't happen to me."

The new evidence indicates that both competent and incompetent professionals burn out. One's sense of personal and professional competence is only one factor of the overall dream, and its existence is not nearly as important as how it fits with the rest of the package. Similarly, higher levels of professional education do not create professionals who are less prone to burnout. While training may increase competence and thus lower the difficulty level at work, in itself it will not prevent burnout.

Vulnerability to stress is often cited as a precursor of burnout. "Look at John; he's all stressed out. I wonder how long he can last," might be a typical statement in many workplaces. John, however, may be the least likely person to become ill, and the person who assumes that he or she has very low stress vulnerability may be the one who suffers the heart attack next week. This may be because we have not understood what really contributes to stress. We usually have defined stressful situations because of the responses of individuals to those situations. What we have been ignoring is the reality that the individual is really manifesting a stressful reaction to a given situation because of interior dissonance which has little to do with the actual external situation.

Those who have chronic health conditions, which means they have to struggle every day, are also not necessarily more likely to develop disabling illness than those who seem to be in good health. Similarly, some of those with happy personal relationships and supportive families become ill, while about equal proportions of those with troubled personal lives burn out.

The reality is that there are many systemic factors, that decline is predictable, that denial is often operating in the minds of the vulnerable, and that the line between health and illness is fragile. Researchers in the Alberta study were startled to discover that teachers who were described as "healthy" by colleagues had profiles dangerously close to those who were on stress leave. What also became clear was that the teachers were not well prepared to assess their risk level for, or recover from, the burnout experience.

At the heart of the experience was often the sense of the *broken dream*. As we will explain later in this book, it is not so much the constant work which burns people out, as the qualities of the dream which drives the caregiver or the inability of that dream to thrive within the system in which he has invested it. That is the soil in which the seeds of hope or despair are planted.

PARTNERSHIP RESPONSIBILITY: THE INSTITUTION AND THE INDIVIDUAL

To assume that the individual is solely responsible for burnout is to blame the victim. To assume the stance that the institution is solely responsible is to place change substantially outside of our power. The increasing recognition that the individual and the institution are partners in the process of sustaining or depleting professionals is a first step to joining personal efforts with systemic changes to create relevant, viable, healthy dreams.

Illness does not come to any person in isolation. The burnout problem, which is growing among caring professionals, has definite systemic factors. By this we mean that in order to have the kind of dream which will motivate and sustain one through the rigors of professional life in today's world, there needs to be systems within which one can appropriately live out those dreams. More and more, systems are compelling caring professionals to compromise their dreams in painful ways. When this happens, the people in the system are ripe for burnout.

Burnout does not happen overnight. Signs and symptoms appear long before the grand fall. Were they recognized earlier, more could be done to prevent a crash. By the time some of the precursor symptoms are recognized, the traditional ways of trying to help, such as "stress management" and fitness programs likely will have little effect. What is needed at this time are interventions which help those affected to reform their dreams or develop new ones.

In reading Tony's case at the beginning of this chapter, if you thought he was very likely to become ill, you were right. The important question is not whether he will burn out, but why?

Did you answer that his over-investment in his work and less involvement with his family was a reason for burnout? If so, you noted a symptom of developing burnout, rather than an underlying cause.

In Tony's case, the combination of factors was more important than anything else. Tony's dream did not have the flexibility to work within the systems in which it was invested. And he unrealistically expected that other members of his family would invest in his dream, rather than needing to follow their own life visions.

If Tony truly wanted to make changes, he would face the challenge of letting go of some of his need to control the dreams of his daughter. He would need to reassess his place within the whole health care system, deciding if he needed to find new ways of being a caregiver, or of working for realistic systemic change.

This book will examine the ways dreams, both corporate and personal, are forged, healthy and unhealthy ways they may be integrated into the lives of professional caregivers, and the potential for examining and restructuring those which are not working.

What would the world be like if we could encourage all our children to create and harness the power of healthy dreams? What if the marketplace learned that its most important cargiving resource was men and women excited and willing to work for a dream? What if corporate dreams, in their turn, were broad and flexible enough to encourage the continued commitment and creativity of these excited caregivers? The potential is unlimited!

QUESTIONS FOR REFLECTION:
DISCOVERING THE DREAMS

We are all visionaries; most of us just have not had a chance to allow that part of ourselves to really be creative. This is a moment to pamper yourself. Find a quiet spot—perhaps in a park or natural environment, or perhaps in your home, with music you enjoy. Choose a time when you will not be disturbed.

You deserve this time to yourself, to allow your visionary side to surface.

When you are ready, take a pen and paper and answer the following questions. Write without worrying about perfectly formed sentences and paragraphs. Our visionary side tends to work much more comfortably when allowed to articulate itself in its own way. You may find yourself writing single words, poetry, or even drawing pictures. Just allow your pen to move across the page in whatever way you respond to the questions.

This is not a time for analysis. Let your mind be non-evaluative, without needing to figure out deep implications to your responses. Just let them happen.

1. What are some of the dreams I had for my life as I was growing up?
2. Have some of those early dreams come true?
3. Are there any of those early dreams which have not come true, but which I would still like to bring into reality?
4. What are some of the corporate, or group, dreams in which I have invested my life? Which parts of these dreams have been fulfilling for me and which have not?
5. If I could write a fairy tale "happily ever after" story for the rest of my life, what would be some of its components? Who would be in it? Who would not be in it? Would I work? If so, what kind of jobs might I have? Would I develop new hobbies or interests, or further develop old ones?

CHAPTER 2

The Anatomy of Dreams

> Reach for the moon and you may be surprised to find your-
> self standing on a star!
>
> *Old Proverb*

What we call a dream—the motivating vision of a person's life—is a very complex tapestry woven through with threads from many sources and of many textures. In reality, few people ever stop and contemplate their own dreams, coming to understand where they came from and their implications. Doing so may not be easy. Honestly contemplating one's dreams may mean confronting painful truths about one's own reality. It may also mean recognizing that there are aspects of the dream which are not working and which, given the reality of one's life, cannot work.

Jack and Cecilia lived in a small community near a large city. He loved his job as a fire fighter and she was happy as a homemaker and mother. For several years, they both felt comfortable that Jack would earn the money for their family.

When their youngest child was in school, Cecilia mentioned to Jack that she would like to attend community college and explore some career options. Jack thought this would be a very good idea. However, with Cecilia's class schedule and Jack's work commitments, it was not long before they realized that childcare would be a problem. Jack found very limited flexibility to his schedule at the fire house. He was not willing to change jobs because he loved his work. Cecilia was thoroughly enjoying

19

school and believed that it was her turn to do something per-
sonally fulfilling away from home.

Jack knew that his marriage and family life and his career
were both very important components of his dream. He realized
that his professional dream and his personal life were interfering
with each other. He also agreed with Cecilia, who told him she
believed her dreams needed to be honored.

What is Jack's dilemma? What is Cecilia's? Is this anyone's
fault, or simply the result of changing life stages? Is there a way
Jack and Cecilia might have avoided this situation? What needs
to happen?

DREAM DIMENSIONS

A dream that has the power to motivate is very different
from a simple expectation. Within any dream may rest many
expectations. A dream, however, holds another dimension.
While expectations are logical; dreams are visionary.

"Reach for the moon, and you may be surprised to find yourself standing on a star!" This is a dream statement. It says, "You
can do wonderful things. Your vision is worth reaching for."

"Nathan will graduate from university and go into the family
business." This is an expectation. If Nathan, however, is able to
envision major growth in the business with himself as the creative force behind the growth, then he can turn the expectation
into a dream.

A dream has energy. It motivates and propels. Dreams can
make waking in the morning a delightful experience and can
sustain individuals and nations through great hardship. If the
dream is a healthy one, sustained by the realities of the world in
which it exists, it energizes to such an extent that in hard times
it can be the difference between success and failure.

Dreams, however, are not always healthy. There is a
large unconscious component to the personal dreams of most
individuals—a component which is not understood, and which,
unexamined, can lead to intense pain. That is why it is important to take the time to examine one's life dream and understand whether it is working with or against you.

There are dreams for many different parts of our lives. One of the most difficult tasks for developing a balanced life is our need to integrate all those dreams into one whole. The ways in which many people live out their dreams resembles an orchestra in which the percussion and brass sections drown out the strings and woodwinds. The result is a cacophony, rather than a symphony, of sound. There is no balance in the presentation. Similarly, a life lived based on a dream which is unbalanced will feel dissonant. Dreams for career, interpersonal relationships, personal development, and play all need to contribute to the larger vision, be acknowledged, and given time and energy.

There are also dreams for different times of life. Think back to your high school days. What were the dreams you had at that time? And as you graduated from university and graduate school, what did you dream for your life? Have you thought about dreams for retirement? As we move through life, our dreams are continuously amended and each time this happens, we need to allow ourselves a small period of grieving for the dreams that were. Some aspects of those dreams, inevitably, were never accomplished. Living healthfully means acknowledging the disappointment, and being ready to let go of unfulfilled dreams whose time has run out, so we can reinvest in today's reality and dreams. Being kind to ourselves in this way will allow us to invest in the reality of our own growth and the aspects of new dreams which will develop.

SHARING DREAMS

We each need to negotiate balance between the many parts of our dreams. When anyone chooses to share his or her life with another person, renegotiation is necessary to build a shared dream as a couple.

There are times in family life when the balance will shift. Choosing to have children may be part of the shared dream, but this choice will ensure the need for changes in the nature or timing of some other dream aspects. Often, when children are small, more dream energy may be invested in those relationships and less in career plans. For many couples, there is an ongoing struggle over the compromises necessary to incorporate the career aspirations of both persons into their shared dream. One member of the couple may not realize that his or her career dream is taking prominence, risking the loss of the other partner's dream. This can deeply stress a relationship. Not surprisingly, one-third of professional women have chosen not to have children. Many men are also rejecting the dream of a traditional family.

From the age of five, Angela can remember having a life vision which included marriage and parenting as well as a fulfilling career. "I firmly believe that a person can do and have it all," she often said. Trained as a clinical social worker, Angela quickly progressed professionally until she was the director of a large department in the mental health program of a major city. She had been dating Jose for three years and they both believed they loved each other.

Angela awoke on her thirty-fifth birthday with a feeling of panic. She looked around her at the home she had created and examined her life. Suddenly, she had a feeling of emptiness. "My biological clock was ticking and I wanted to move on and make real some more components of my life dream—marriage and children."

That evening, she told Jose how she was feeling and asked him if he felt the same. He replied that he was very happy with the current status of his relationship. He was not interested in picket fences and strollers.

Angela decided that it was time for her to follow her own dream. She ended her relationship with Jose and began looking for another relationship which could lead to marriage. Jose became deeply depressed. He finally contacted a counselor and at their first session together, he repeated over and over that his life had fallen apart when Angela had left him. He could not believe that he had contributed to that breakup because he had always tried to treat her well.

Angela agreed to come to a session with him, where she told him that their breakup was not because of anything he had done, but was about her need to move on and embrace other dream aspects of her life. His dream did not have those aspects, so she needed to move on without him. As they began to share deeply about their dreams, both of them decided to try again with their relationship, and to spend more time considering each other's dreams. A year later they were married and another year later, Angela gave birth to twin boys. They never did move to suburbia and picket fences; they continued to maintain a city lifestyle. They did move to a larger apartment near a park. Jose is a doting father, and the addition of an excellent nanny has enabled both parents to maintain their careers while not neglecting their children.

Angela and Jose were able to develop a shared dream which would creatively embrace aspects of both their life visions.

THE DREAMING SPIRIT

We don't think out our dreams. They are not an intellectual exercise. They arise from our spirits.

Spirit means different things to different people. We are using it to mean both one's sense of the infinite and the part of oneself that is the most authentic and real. Have you ever seen a Russian doll—the kind with several layers nestled within each other? Our sense of who we are is very much like those dolls. For each of us, the strong, solid little doll in the center is *me*. As I grew, I gradually learned from society, my parents, and teachers, new ways to define myself, new life expectations, and roles. Layer upon layer was added to my sense of who I was. Gradually, that strong inner sense of me became buried in more and more layers of *me as I have learned to be.*

If you take apart a Russian doll, you see that each layer is made of very thin wood. Individually, they could each be easily crushed. The small, solid inner doll, however, is very stable and strong. What it lacks in size, it makes up for in strength. The part of a person which corresponds to this small inner doll may be the part that will exist when the body has decayed. It may be the "who one is" that other people see when they look into your open eyes. Many people believe that it is from this place within that one communicates with the Holy. We could call it the "soulplace."

Sadly, this part of oneself has often been lost. When this happens, the person becomes like the Russian doll without its central character. There is a place of emptiness at this person's center. Realization of this emptiness often brings people into counseling. The journey of therapy is variously described as finding a missing part of myself," "coming home to myself," or "centering my life." This journey involves finding the missing parts of oneself and placing them into the empty space, then learning to discern the true voice of oneself from that soulplace within and separating it from all the other voices we hear that tell us we need to look outside ourselves for life satisfaction.

For many people, the spirit is the seat of creativity. It is in learning to listen to the voice of this part of ourselves that we are energized for the more pragmatic and external aspects of honoring our life dreams.

THE GENDERED DREAM

It would be wonderful if all one had to do was to hook into the authentic voice within, and then go out and live that dream. Realistically, however, we must acknowledge that cultural attitudes will affect both the development of any dream and also how it is lived out.

Society strongly influences dreams. Many aspects of personal dreams are actually pre-scripted by the expectations of others. Within society, there are very different expectations for male and female roles. The more one is influenced by these role expectations, the more likely one's dreams will not be authentically one's own. Research shows that while society expects women to invest themselves in the caretaking roles of being wives and mothers, it is actually men who experience stronger satisfaction with married life than women. With each child's birth, the satisfaction level lowers for women and increases for men. We believe that this reality comes about directly because of society's dreams for women and the fact that it is very difficult for girls and women to go against the mainstream and stand up for their own interests instead of caring for others.

While Melanie was working on her Ph.D. in psychology, she had two children. The next year, just a few months into her new career, she found that she was pregnant again. Melanie became deeply depressed, nearly immobilized by the realization that while she had worked so hard to attain the goal of professional preparation, the other side of her life was in chaos. Her husband, Jim, did not understand why she did not want to simply stay home and care for the family. He was a successful businessman and could support them financially. He traveled a great deal on business and thought that the children needed their mother to be home.

Melanie found a nanny and worked part-time. She loved her children and being their mother. She also loved her work and she perceived that unless she could invest a few years into high energy career development, she would not be able to maintain her impetus in a very competitive field.

Melanie was in the double bind experienced by many women who want successful careers. If she worked as much as she believed was required, she could be accused of neglecting her children. If she spent more time on parenting, her career would suffer and her career was very important to her sense of self.

Melanie was all the more frustrated by the fact that Jim could apply most of his energy to his career and very little to his family relationships and still be seen by society as an excellent father.

It seems obvious that women, partly because of their biological structure and partly because of societal expectations, struggle constantly to balance their personal and professional lives. On the other hand, while the reality is that males are most often in control in our society, there is also much more pressure on males to conform to their role models. Any minor divergence in dress or behavior is experienced as threatening to the stereotypical male self-image. So, for example, while male teachers are important to young children, society strongly disapproves of this as a suitable career for men. One young man, qualified and deeply wanting to be a kindergarten teacher, could not get a job. He could never get an explanation about why he was not hired. Finally, a principal said to him, "We really think a woman would be better with these small children."

THE PRE-SCRIPTED LEGACY DREAM

Personal dreams arise from many sources. Many people live their lives through pre-scripted dreams inherited from their families or other influential people in their lives. These dreams often involve daily behaviors and values, professional goals, and ideas about relationships and marriage. It is amazing how few people ever examine their reasons for making major life decisions.

Western society does not encourage contemplation. In an age when more and more life possibilities are opening up for young people, we still ask young children, "What do you want to be when you grow up?" A dozen children were asked that very question. Ten of the twelve immediately looked at their parents before answering the question. Three actually asked their parents to answer for them. Four parents felt obligated to explain and interpret their children's answers. Watching these interactions was an interesting demonstration of the subtle and not-so-subtle ways most of us have been programmed by our parents' dreams and needs.

Tony, whose story was told in Chapter 1, had developed his life dream out of the ethic of his immigrant, war-torn family. He assumed that he could hand on to his children the values inherent in that dream. When that did not happen, Tony's dream began to fall apart.

What parent has not held their newborn child and dreamed for him or her a future rosy with whatever is dear to the parent? We all want "the best" for our children. Unfortunately, what parents interpret as being "THE best" is often "OUR OWN best," based on the parents' values and interests. Few of us stop to realize that the newly-born person has a right to his or her own values and interests, which may be very different from our own.

Often, the dreams which parents invest in their children have a great deal to do with areas of life in which the parents feel deficient—things they wish they had done or had been able to do. Sometimes, they involve actual failures which the parents have experienced. If their children can succeed where they have failed, it will seem as if the parents themselves vicariously have another chance.

Just as often, parents have found great satisfaction or fulfillment from certain activities or values, and presume that their children will derive the same level of pleasure from a life similar to their own.

Right from the beginning, often before they can speak their own thoughts, children are being programmed with values and ideas which excite their primary caregivers, usually their parents. This happens so smoothly that most of us do not even realize it is happening. Unfortunately, a sense of one's personal identity is very slow in forming, and it is often when people are well into adult life that they realize that they are not really living what they would have chosen for themselves.

James was the third son of an Irish-American family. He was the son dedicated to God. There was never any question in the family that James would become a priest.

When he was thirteen years old, James was sent to a boarding school especially for boys contemplating priesthood—one of those institutions, many of which have now been abandoned, which formed the chain of Roman Catholic "minor seminaries" in the United States. He was a bright boy and a good student, and the program was carefully designed so the boys received praise only for "appropriate" grades and behaviors. When James would visit his home for vacations, there would always be celebrations and parties which reinforced the "special" nature of James' vocation. To be "called by God" was the highest honor a young man could have. To be the parents of a priest would assure his parents a plush spot in heaven for eternity, not to mention a great deal of approval and attention in this life.

Several of James' friends decided to leave the seminary life before ordination. When this happened, James heard from his teachers and family, "How could he let down his family and God like that? What a selfish decision!" James was not a selfish person, and he wanted to please both his family and God. At the age of twenty-seven, he was ordained a priest and set out for his first ministry as assistant in a large city parish.

Although he did not particularly enjoy being low man on the hierarchy, especially after a lifetime of being told how special he was, James knew that as a young priest, he had to pay his dues. He learned very well how to play the games of the institution through which his life was lived. He learned what the rules really meant. He distinguished himself on several fronts and rose quickly through the political structures of his church. Well before he was middle-aged, he was pastor of a thriving parish and a frequent consultant to church leadership in issues of moral theology.

James seemed to have reached the pinnacle of his dream. His family was astounded when he visited them in the fall of his forty-second year and told them that he would be applying to leave the priesthood. No, he did not want to be married—at least, not at the moment. But he had never been happy within himself, and he needed to build a life dream of his own.

Visiting his family and giving them that news was the most difficult thing James had ever done. He was not angry with God. In fact, he wanted very much to serve God in his life. Through therapy over the past two years, he had realized that there were many ways he could do that, and that he needed to listen to his own heart and do it his own way.

His parents, of course, had a very difficult time accepting his decision. It is hard to see one's child grow up and discard the dream one has bequeathed to that child. James' pain, however, had become so strong that he could no longer live his parents' dream, even though he did not want to disappoint them. He had entered therapy because of headaches, digestive problems, and allergies which did not respond to medical treatment. After many months of therapy, when he had finally begun to accept his right to his own dream, the physical symptoms lessened, flaring up again as the time approached to tell his family. Once he had done that, and could get on with his life, he was physically quite well, experiencing only occasional headaches or mild allergy symptoms.

THE REBEL'S DREAM

There is another group of people who are living dreams strongly influenced by their parents, although many would vehemently deny that fact. These are the rebels, who in rebelling against the "legacy dreams" given them by their parents, instead choose to live as differently as possible from what they think their parents would want. This situation is just the other side of the coin of the pre-scripted legacy dream. These people are not living dreams which they chose because of personal preference, but ones they rushed into because of anger and rebellion. Their dreams are no more integrated into their personalities than those which would allow their parents to live vicariously through them. Neither situation honors the unique person living the dream. Neither dream is authentic.

SOCIETAL INFLUENCES ON DREAM FORMATION

Society too, helps to script our dreams. Teachers are tremendously influential in teaching children about their potential or lack of potential, and in sharing their own values with their students.

There is no value-free educational system. Often, which values are transmitted is the choice of the classroom teacher. Teachers, like the rest of us, are often unable to support each student in accessing his or her unique experience to form personal values. Even if teachers present many options, values are so foundational in our lives that we will be influenced one way or another by the personal attitudes and values of our teachers.

The media, literary and film, possibly has more influence on human behavior than any other single agent. While very few people would intentionally watch television or movies to learn how to behave, the fact is that behaviors are learned from watching others. It is often difficult to recognize the difference between fantasy and reality. Parents in the midwest who watch television shows about teens in Beverly Hills (mainly played by adult actors) are learning how to relate to their children. Children and teens watch television and find out which social behaviors are appropriate. These plastic images become part of the life scripts for whole families. Often, because these fantasy scripts are written to entertain, not to teach, they have very little relevance to real life. Because television characters come into our homes so often, they become nearly like members of the family. The values of a television show can become the values of a family! If television says, " I must become wealthy to be successful," or, "Only in certain professions will I achieve prestige," that message may very well influence life decisions. For example, for several years the media has painted scientific people as "nerds," and universities across North America have found a deficit in the number of students entering programs like engineering and mathematics/physics. These professions, as portrayed in the media, are *not cool*.

THE TIMING OF DREAMS

It is clear that the values and ideals of people other than oneself may have a very strong impact upon the formation of one's life dream. In fact, it is unusual for a young adult to have much of his or her own personal essence in the life dream with which he or she first faces adult life. This is because most people in their early twenties are still not very aware of and confident in their own unique identities. Think about yourself. The first time you could vote, did you research the candidates and decide how to vote according to your own preference? Or did you automatically vote according to the political preference of some influential older person, or of your peer friends? Or perhaps you just stayed away from the polls because you did not feel able to decide from within your own resources. If you fit into the first group, those who were able to vote autonomously, you were an especially mature person, unusual among your age group.

Most young adults simply do not understand enough about life or about themselves to know how to form their own unique personally-integrated life dreams. It is often not until the fourth decade of life that most people really begin to get in touch with their own authentic personalities, and personal insight grows slowly thereafter, as long as one lives.

Usually, people start by trying to make real and live out a dream that is based on something not authentically their own. When they realize that fact, something deep within themselves cries out to be recognized and lived. A thirty-seven-year-old teacher told his family that he needed to resign as head of the History Department of a large high school. He was returning to university to study psychology. Something within him was demanding that he notice and change his professional life vision.

A woman who had been a teaching sister for many years left the convent and changed professions at the age of thirty-three. Asked over and over why she had done such a thing, she would reply, "It's hard to say, but it just didn't seem to fit any more, who I really was. It didn't seem true to myself."

MID-LIFE CRISIS

This realization, that the dream one has been living is not "true to myself," can be terrifying. But if those entering into this stage of development allow themselves to process what they are realizing, and to proceed with discerning their options, it can be a time for major growth and new life excitement. On the other hand, those who do not allow the process to happen often experience a time of frustration, anger, and burnout.

This time in life when many people become aware of their need for personal authenticity, for living the dreams which are their own, has often been labeled "mid-life crisis." People look around at life, look ahead to the amount of time left, and become afraid that they cannot accomplish their goals. Many are not even aware of the nature of their own dreams, although they know that what they have been living is not authentic. One man said, "It's as if something inside me is pushing to be born, but I am half afraid to let it out because I don't know what it will be. I know that, like a woman in labor, I must allow it to have life. But do I have the energy or ability to respond to it when I meet it face to face? I don't know. I am confused and afraid; but I know I must go on."

As we come to that point in life of discovering personal interests and needs, the task is to evaluate the dreams we have been living, finding those factors which work and those which do not. Moving through "mid-life crisis" (whenever it happens!) means undertaking this evaluation, and then allowing oneself to develop a dream which will work. This may mean being brutally realistic about personal talents and the systems within which we live and work. It may mean finding a professional to help with the process. But if the original dreams can be reformulated, or new ones which will work can be developed, the second half of life can take on new meaning and depth of fulfillment.

One reassuring insight is that, although it often seems to the person undertaking this process as if he or she does not have a long time to live out the new dream, once reality has been embraced, most people have a great many skills for moving on which they have been learning throughout their early lives. Some new life skills may be necessary, but most of what is needed is already in place, and many are surprised at how quickly their new dreams begin to gel.

THE NEED FOR CONTROL:
THE DISAPPEARANCE OF PRE-SCRIPTED SECURITY

One of the most difficult situations happens when a person has been living what felt like an authentic life within a system that supports the person's vision, when suddenly the system changes or disappears. A few years ago, when training for professional careers, people were told, "You'll always be in demand. Society can't do without nurses (police officers, doctors, teachers, etc.)." Now, however, many caregivers have been faced with drastic cutbacks or layoffs because of managed care, budget cuts, and other factors beyond personal control.

Cheryl was a psychologist working for twelve years in a large Health Management Organization. One Wednesday afternoon, at a routine department meeting, the administrator of the clinic announced that the HMO was "down-sizing." Half of the positions in the department were to be cut and the other half would become part-time positions. Since Cheryl was a single mother and needed a full-time position, that meant she would need to look for another job. She knew that if she did so, she would lose her seniority and believed that she would have to start all over again to establish herself in a new organization. While she did receive other job offers right away, Cheryl went from one job to another for the next five years, changing every few months. She would always find something wrong with every position.

Cheryl was frustrated and felt as if her life was out of control. Finally, one Monday, she could not get out of bed and go to work. Her sister found her still in bed at 11 A.M. the next morning. Cheryl was profoundly depressed. She needed to work with a therapist to recover her sense of self and her ability to control her own life. She needed to grieve for her sense of trust in the system which let her down, her sense of her own professional security.

QUESTIONS FOR REFLECTION: WHERE AND HOW WERE MY DREAMS CREATED?

EXERCISE—THE FIRST STEP IN EVALUATION

Because the origins of your youthful dreams were likely based upon the values and hopes of influences outside yourself, you may have found that your sense of personal fulfillment is low and your frustration and disappointment level is high.

This frustration and disappointment, if not processed, can build up within your system until you become ill. This condition we call *burnout*.

The first step in processing the frustration and disappointment is to acknowledge that it is there. After you have admitted its existence, you can begin to discern its origins.

1. As I was growing up, who were the most influential people in my life?
2. What are some of the values I live today which I inherited from my parents or other influential adults? Have I taken the time to assess whether or not these values are really important to me personally?
3. As much as I can remember, what were some of the influences I felt in entering my professional field? On a scale of 1 to 10, where 1 is *not at all* and 10 is *very, very strongly*, how much would I say the opinions of others influenced my decision?
4. Have I learned anything about myself as I have grown older which, had I known these things at eighteen, would likely have caused me to choose a different area or style of work?
5. What is important about my time of life in assessing my dream realities at the present moment?
6. How do I feel about my answers to the above questions?

CHAPTER 3

The Dreaming Self

And a man said, Speak to us of Self-Knowledge.
And he answered, saying:
Your hearts know in silence the secrets of your days and nights.
But your ears thirst for the sounds of your heart's knowledge.
You would know in words that which you have always known in thought.
You would touch with your fingers the naked body of your dream,
And it is well you should.
The hidden well-spring of your soul must needs rise and run
murmuring to the sea;
And the treasure of your infinite depths would be revealed to your eyes.
But let there be no scales to weigh your unknown treasures;
And seek not the depths of your knowledge with staff or sounding line.
For self is a sea boundless and measureless.
Say not, "I have found the truth," but rather, "I have found a truth."
Say not, "I have found the path of the soul."
Say rather, "I have met the soul walking upon my path."
For the soul walks upon all paths.
The soul walks neither upon a line, neither does it grow like a reed.
The soul unfolds itself, like a lotus of countless petals.

Kahlil Gibran [1]

LEARNING TO LOSE OUR SENSE
OF OURSELVES

Have you ever watched a baby learn to crawl? She[1] is absolutely sure that if she tries hard enough, she can figure out how to get across the room to Daddy's arms. She will spend long periods and great energy in the process of bringing her commitment to reality. First, she spends a few days learning how to pull her legs under herself, until she's up on her hands and knees. Rocking back and forth, she is amazed that she is still in the

---

[1] We believe in and support the equality of men and women. However, we ask our readers to please accept the outdated "she, he" when it appears in our writing, reflecting either or both genders.

same place. But Daddy smiles and says, "Come on, Baby. You'll figure it out. You can do it!" His words and smile give her the energy to work through the complicated maneuvers which will eventually lead her into Daddy's lap—and the whole world is just one step away!

What would happen to that baby if everyone around told her, "You really don't want to learn to crawl. That's a stupid ambition!" Since we can't be in the mind of an infant, it is impossible to say with certainty. It is, however, likely that the baby would stop her quest and try to invest her interests in some other activity for which she could earn her parents' approval. She would have learned a bitter lesson—I don't have the ability to judge which ambitions are worthwhile. I really don't know what's best for myself. I need to learn to listen to other people who know better than I.

In learning this lesson, our baby would have given away a part of her own *selfhood*—her sense of who she uniquely is and what she can know about her own needs.

It may seem silly to think about parents telling their child not to crawl. After all, crawling is what babies do. It's one of the developmental necessities on the way to life independence. Yet most children are not very old before parents and teachers begin teaching them the same bitter lesson our fictional baby was taught. We all learned, very young, that there were other, older, wiser, smarter people who would interpret life for us and tell us how we should respond. Big people knew what we could and could not, should and should not, do.

When Donna's son, Kevin, was almost five years old, they went for his orientation day at kindergarten. The teacher gave each child a picture of a duck and told them to color their ducks however they wished. There were yellow ducks with orange beaks and feet and gray ducks with red beaks and feet. There were even a few green, purple, and blue ducks—not that different from nature's palate—and then there was Kevin's duck. It was striped, with a purple beak, one foot red, and one foot green. It was the only picture that didn't have any semblance to the real thing. Donna was mortified. The teacher would think she had never taken Kevin to a petting zoo or park! The other parents would know immediately, that she had been an inadequate or deficient parent.

The teacher walked slowly around the table, complimenting each child on his or her work. As she neared Kevin, she began to chuckle. Donna thought, "Oh no! She's going to reject his duck and tease him!" Instead, the teacher picked up Kevin's duck and showed it to the class. "This," she declared, "is a magic duck!" "Why, a duck of many colors like this one is very special indeed! What a wonderful duck Kevin has colored!" All the other children and parents clapped and congratulated Kevin for his imagination and creativity.

That day, Kevin learned a lesson. Donna learned an even more important one about the value and magic of imagination, and about the ways to nurture a child in finding his own unique selfhood and following his own dreams.

Unfortunately, many of us have not been gifted with such a wise teacher, and our parents did not learn that important lesson about nurturing and encouraging. Often, we learned that in order to be acceptable, we needed to stop dreaming, to give up our own ideas, and accept those of authority figures in our lives.

When we learn that lesson, we stop imagining, we stop visioning, and we stop dreaming. Instead, we buy into the dreams of those people we have been taught to respect. We become passive and agreeable and move away from our selfhood and into a sense of reality acquired from others. We refrain from writing our own life stories and become chapters amended to the stories of others.

This process of molding children into shapes selected by their parents, teachers, and churches has happened, to some degree, to everyone. Those who will not be molded are labeled— *uncooperative—rebellious—impossible*—and are nudged to the periphery of society.

Fourteen-year-old Jennifer was detained by the security officer at the neighborhood drug store. She was taken to a back room and accused of shoplifting. In spite of her protests that she was innocent, her parents were called. When they arrived, the security officer ordered her to empty her purse on the desk. Only her personal possessions fell out of the purse. The officer took the purse and peered into its depth, looking for stolen materials. Nothing could be found because Jennifer had not stolen anything, that day or any other.

When her parents asked the officer why she had been detained, he said it was because of the way she looked. Jennifer had bright pink hair and a ring in her nostril. She wore army boots and a long shapeless dress and her lips were painted black.

"You see, we've had a rash of shoplifting lately, and we're cracking down on these kids," said the officer to justify his behavior.

Jennifer waited for her parents to defend her, to tell the officer that they knew their daughter would not steal.

Instead, they turned to her with an 'I told you so' look on their faces. "If you wouldn't look like a thief, you wouldn't be in trouble," said her father.

The family walked out of the store and went home without any conversation. Jennifer had learned her lesson well. The next day, she dyed her hair its natural brown color and took the ring out of her nose. Ten years later, she graduated with a Master's degree in education. Three years into her teaching career, Jennifer developed acute migraine headaches which incapacitated her several days a month. Her problem was so severe that she took a leave from teaching and went into therapy.

Jennifer's story is not about whether teenagers should or should not have nose rings and pink hair. It is about one child's quest to write her own story, to find her real self. It is about the ways she was blocked from doing so because her parents and others in society could not allow her to explore the possibilities. When she entered therapy, Jennifer had no sense of who she was. When her therapist asked her questions, she would parrot an answer she had learned from someone else. She had forgotten how to find her own truth. Finally one day, she shouted, "No! That's not what I believe. I believe . . ." Try as she would, she could not find her own belief within herself. Jennifer plunged into a chasm of unknowing. With encouragement, she explored the crevices and knolls within that chasm until she found her own answers and was able to climb, by then, onto firm ground.

By the time we are ready to enter college, other people's visions and values have become the directives for our lives. Like the spirit of a horse, we may have been broken gently or cruelly. Nevertheless, we are driven by reins we do not control. To varying degrees, our spirits are broken or controlled. When human spirits are broken, souls are depleted. We lose our own voices, speaking learned messages. We tell and live other people's stories.

Usually, parents are not to blame. The role of parents is to provide values and direction during our formative years. The difficulty arises when we fail to assess our early training in light of our adult lives. Some of the messages we have learned are good ones. Many of them are messages of service, caring, and love—of independence and leadership. Few messages in and of themselves are unhealthy. It is in the embracing of them so fully that we see no other way of being, that we become unprepared for the full range of human experiences. We feel a gap somewhere deep inside. We hunger for a wholeness that eludes us. We are ill-equipped for the hard journey of contemporary professional life.

We have become like the Russian doll with its small, but important, central figure missing—having many layers, but with an empty space where the strong little soul doll should fit at its center.

REFINDING OUR SELVES

The task of becoming whole and strong involves exploring and perhaps rewriting our own stories, to refind our souls and listen to them, hearing the wisdom that comes from deep inside ourselves (see [2], it provides a very helpful approach to examining the genesis and unfolding of one's life).

One of the difficulties of finding meaning in life is that we are taught many things that do not necessarily contribute to meaning or to survival. The world we live in says, "Here is what to hope for. Here are the rules. Follow these and you'll be OK." Some listen to this advice and strive to excel. Others are defeated along the way. Still others decide not to even play the game, thinking, "I can't win, anyway." Then, just when you think you've got it figured out to the point that you feel it will work for you and you have a reasonable chance at success, the rules change.

We are bombarded with advice about setting directions and meeting goals, and told that it is crucial to have goals and hopes for the future. Absolutely crucial. Life, however, is sometimes not about achieving successes to which others can point. Sometimes we need to set goals for *who we are*—the kind of people we are in the world—*not just what we do*. In this chapter, we invite you to set goals for your selfhood as well as for your career.

Defining in clear language what *a self* is seems to be an impossible task. Many have tried and we are not aware of anyone who has succeeded completely.

At this point in the book, we wanted to write a very wise and astute treatise which would guide you, our readers, toward a sudden depth of insight and personal understanding. We found though, that the more deeply we went into the question of *self*, the more questions we found. Each person's insight will be unique, arising out of his or her own story. Within our stories are many different selves, and we know ourselves differently through differing experiences.

We believe that knowing one's *self* must be experiential. It means exploring and rewriting our life stories, having the courage and the freedom to venture down many roads until we find the path that feels right, that *fits*. When we undertake this adventure, we discover things that each of us can only know about ourselves. We can say, as Kahlil Gibran's prophet did, "I have found the soul walking on my path."

Possibly, there are many truths for each person. We know when we have found truth of our own, and after that discovery, nobody can take it from us. With each discovery, our story becomes more real. We become more authentic and we can dream dreams that are uniquely right for ourselves.

As we have been writing this book, in our search for ways to define *self*, we came across the attempts of several people who have also struggled with the concept of *self*, particularly in relation to life story. We offer some of them here for your reflection.

> We can get along without our souls for a little while in life, but not for long [3, p. 108].

Our tragedies, our triumphs, our pain, our hopes are the fingerprints of our souls. (*Jevne; personal journal*)

Story is the only thing we have at the end of our lives, and it is everything [2, p. 50].

There is in each of us an ongoing story. It contains our meaning and our destiny. And it goes on inevitably whether we pay attention to it or not. This is our "soul story" . . . A self is made, not given. It is a creative and active process of attending a life that must be heard, shaped, seen, said aloud into the world, finally enacted and woven into the lives of others [2, p. 50].

Metzger reminds us that stories heal us because we become whole through them. In the process of writing, of discovering our story, we "restory" those parts of ourselves that have been scattered, hidden, suppressed, denied, distorted, and forbidden, and we come to understand that stories heal. As in the word *remember*, we re-member; we bring together the parts. We integrate that which has been alienated or separated out; revalue what has been disdained. In other words, self-discovery is more than gathering information about oneself. The gathering—the coming to know—has consequences. It alters us. We re-store, re-member, re-vitalize, re-juvenate, rescue, re-cover, re-claim, and re-new. Writing our story takes us back to some early time when we were emotionally and spiritually whole.

This quest for our unique stories—the search for self—is not an exercise to solve life's dilemmas. In finding our souls, we will not resolve problems like injustice, lack of love, powerlessness, or disability. In fact, those who have explored before us, tell us that the mystery of the story becomes deeper as we move closer to our own truth.

It may seem as if the quest is futile. Not so! There are certain life journeys for which the journey itself is the reason. In this case, the journey is about you! Even the questions which seem to have no answers will help you understand yourself. Your questions will be your own, and will only make sense to you. And in understanding the difference between your questions and those of others, you will come to understand yourself.

The greatest scientists of the world, in their quest for answers, continue to discover more and more insoluble mysteries. Generation after generation, they move closer to understanding the universe. Generation after generation, they learn more about the insoluble. In spite of this reality, what they have learned has been invaluable. Through their quests, they have also found much which is untrue, and the exposing of those untruths has often been as important as the finding of truth.

As we undertake a journey to find our own unique truths, we will without doubt begin to expose what is not true in the stories others have written for us. And on the other side of each untruth will be a personal truth, which can be rewoven into the real story. At some point in the real story, our souls begin to speak with their own voices, becoming louder and louder as we explore more and more deeply. And finally, our souls will speak forth ourselves, and we will meet the world's dilemmas garbed in our own truths. What we do not know—what we cannot solve—will become less important because we will know what we do know. Our real stories provide a firm foundation for our lives.

While we hope to inspire you, our readers, with excitement to explore and rewrite your own life narratives, we do so realizing that it will take immense courage and faith to begin this quest. Many of us have so deeply learned to only understand ourselves through old stories, often written by others, that a state of inertia disempowers us from moving on. There are very real dangers to moving away from the comfortable, especially if large parts of the familiar self-story are about our own fears, misgivings, limitations, or disabilities. Powerful questions begin to gather at the fork in the road, building barriers to our exploration. "What if I find that I am really inadequate? What if the truths I find are frightening, or call me into areas of life which I fear? What if I find nothing—proof that I am nobody"?

Other people may block the pathways, especially those who have been most influential in writing our familiar stories. They may be hurt that we do not accept the stories they have told about us. Equally possible, they may feel afraid that when we become ourselves, they will not know us and will lose us. Often in our quest, we discover that we are angry with these people but have never expressed or worked through that anger.

For many people, there comes a point at which they meet this anger crouched beside their pathway. They know that the anger is about the ways other people, often people they love, have controlled the writing of their stories. The anger is a very powerful force and threatens to ambush them and overpower their journeys. Sometimes people abandon the search at this point. Others sit down beside the path and spend great stretches of time playing games with the anger but never really confronting it.

There are many, however, who stop and enter into a dialogue with the anger. These people realize that it is only in finding their own voices, that they can love themselves. They recognize that only when they love themselves, can they love others.

There is no question that this undertaking can be disturbing. We encourage you to acknowledge your fears and initiate a dialogue with them. Remember, the fears are invested in your not moving on. They want you to stay in the place you were when you bought this book. However, the fact that you did buy the book indicates that you are feeling uncomfortable in that familiar place. Some things are not working. You are looking for alternatives. Your fears are grounded in the status quo. You may feel ready to move into a time of change. Perhaps you don't feel ready but life is propelling you toward change. Recognize and acknowledge your fears. This will lessen their power. Refuse to allow them to block your life pathway.

Some people find that it is useful to invite their fears to journey awhile with them. They promise to move slowly, until the fears can become accustomed to the gradual changes.

It's OK to be afraid. That is a natural human response to change. It is only when we allow the fears to overpower us and prevent the journey that fearfulness becomes oppressive.

In addressing and acknowledging our fears, we also begin to find hope for the journey. In finding courage to acknowledge and own our fears, we realize that we can also find courage to move further along the path. Unacknowledged, overpowering fear is often paralyzing, preventing any forward life movement. Taking control of valid fears begins to open up possibilities. It works something like the way physical therapy and heat will begin to heal atrophied muscles when a cast is removed. For some, this may be painful at first, but the movement will gradually become more fluid and comfortable. Forward movement into the quest may at first be halting and tenuous, but each new step will propel us forward into the excitement of the journey. There is so much to be discovered! Hope grows as we learn to believe in the journey.

This is a journey of hope!

QUESTIONS FOR REFLECTION: VALUING MYSELF

1. Do you remember what you looked like as a child? Find an old photograph and look at it. How do you experience yourself? How much of the way you see yourself in that photograph has been influenced by what others have taught you? (Donna, for example, hated looking at childhood photographs because she only saw a skinny, freckled urchin, never a sweet little Irish-Canadian girl.) Now, try to look at that photograph through the eyes of someone who loved you and thought you were a perfect child—perhaps a grandparent or a favorite aunt or uncle. Does this change the way you see yourself?

2. Recall a situation when you sensed that who you were was not acceptable or appropriate. Who was there? What was the situation? How did you know that you were not OK? Can you remember what you decided? How have incidents like that influenced the storying of your life?

3. Who were three important people in your life as you were growing up? If they were describing you as a child, what would they have said? How has each of their messages influenced the way you perceive yourself?

4. Can you describe any ideas or behaviors which do not feel right for you but which you have adopted into your personal or professional life?

5. Can you describe any ideas or behaviors which feel like a true fit for your life, and which you have been living. What is it about these ideas or behaviors that feels so comfortable?

6. From what you know about yourself today, if you were living a life that felt true to yourself, what might you be trying, doing, and speaking?

7. If you really begin the quest for self—the re-storying of your life—what people will support you? Who might oppose this quest? Why have you chosen these people for each category?

8. What do you think might motivate those who might oppose your quest for personal truth? Would they be afraid that they will lose their relationships with you? What part of them is invested in your old story? Is there some way you can invite them to be part of the re-storying, always remembering that you are now the author?

9. Are you, yourself, afraid of the journey? Why? Allow yourself to acknowledge this fear, if it exists. Try to understand what it arises from, the source of the fear. Write it down— "I am afraid of . . . because. . . ."

10. Now, write down the reasons to begin the journey. What is hopeful for you? (Be aware that your fears may try to prevent you from acknowledging your hopes.) What do you stand to gain through this quest?

REFERENCES

1. K. Gibran, *The Prophet,* Alfred A. Knopf, 1964.
2. Sr. D. Metzger, *Writing For Your Life: A Guide and Companion to the Inner Worlds,* Harper, San Francisco, 1992.
3. W. Lynch, *Images of Hope: Imagination as Healer of the Hopeless,* Mentor-Omega, The New American Library, New York, 1965.

CHAPTER 4

Living the Dream:
The Blessing and the Curse

It isn't a bad thing to be a dreamer,
provided you are awake when you dream [1, p. 88].

Why is it that some dreams translate into real life and effective actions, while others bring only frustration? In reality, there are many people whose childhood dreams flower and bear the fruits of fulfillment and satisfaction for the caregiver as well as enriching the lives of others.

When Marcus was seven years old, he had his tonsils out. From that day on, he wanted to be a doctor. He dreamed of no other professional possibilities. Sure enough, his dream, plus a lot of hard work, led him into a satisfying and rewarding adult life. He married Felice, also a physician, and they found appropriate ways to share their dreams of professional and personal fulfillment. Last year, they both retired and are enjoying their grandchildren and various travel and sports hobbies.

Marcus, Felice, and others like them illustrate that one's dreams can nourish and support a satisfying life.

Others seem to "fall into" professional careers without much forethought, and those places where they land, end up fitting as if they were created for just that person. Janet says, "When I entered college, I had no idea of what I wanted to do. But I found that I did very well in psychology courses. I ended up being a clinical psychologist. I love my work and the life opportunities it offers me."

For others, the longed-for satisfaction and fulfillment seem elusive and the chase to find them, exhausting. One young woman in her third year of teaching asked, "Why isn't it happening for me when it happens for people all around me?" When asked what she meant by "happening," she explained that her colleagues seemed to find satisfaction and even joy in their work, while she experienced only frustration. Her personal life was much the same. Things just didn't come together the way she had dreamed.

Another woman, a nurse for fifteen years, said that she had to force herself to go to work each day, because it was not at all the way she wanted it to be, and no matter how hard she tried to be a competent and compassionate nurse, she felt as if she was "out of step" with the system, her colleagues, and even many of her patients.

"The system cuts corners and values dollars more than people. Most other nurses seem to have accommodated to the system, or they're just doing whatever is necessary to hold onto their jobs. And the patients know they're not getting what they should because of budget cutbacks. They're paying more than ever for care, but receiving less services. So they're crabby with the nurses—which makes the nurses turn off all the more."

Why is it that some people with commendable dreams end up feeling like this? What can we do, as caregivers, to retain our own strength and sense of fulfillment, and to support our colleagues? How can we prevent ourselves from lapsing into self-blame when our dreams stop working?

DREAMS THAT NOURISH

Dreams that nourish life and fulfillment are those which emanate from the soulplace and speak the unique insights of the individual. They do not speak with the voices of other people, but with the clear voice of self-awareness.

Faith was thirty-three years old, the divorced parent of four children. Her ex-husband had brutally abused her and then thrown her and the children out of their house. A year later, she met Tom. He was a kind and gentle man and the children loved him. He wanted to marry Faith and "take care of her."

When Faith was with him, however, she felt herself struggling to maintain an interest in the things which interested him. One day, she realized that she found him boring. He was not interested in community or world affairs. He had little professional ambition, while she was struggling through university.

Faith's family said, "Don't let him get away. He'll always be good to you and the children. He's stable and caring."

The dissonance between what others were saying and what her own soul was telling her was strong enough that Faith sought professional guidance from a counselor. When the counselor asked her what her own heart was saying, she replied, "I can't marry him. His dream will stifle my soul. I need to follow my own dream."

Five years later, as Faith was completing her second year as a teacher, she said, "I'm so glad I followed my own dream. Even though it seemed like the most difficult road to take at the time, it has led me into a place in life where I feel whole and excited about the future."

DREAMS THAT DEPLETE

The symptoms of burnout are the symptoms of broken dreams. Participants in the Alberta study reported a growing feeling of *becoming less* as they approached burnout—less enthusiastic, less idealistic, less valued, less able, less in control, and less connected to others. These feelings are sad and frightening, and people who experience these feelings usually either try frantically to make things work, or withdraw and stop trying. The following vignette tells about a person whose soul had lost its own voice and was speaking through the voices of other people.

Jason was a seventeen-year-old eleventh-grade student whose parents brought him to family counseling because he was failing every subject and the school had threatened to ask him to leave. During the first session, Jason sat sullenly in the counseling office. His parents quickly revealed why they were there.

"He doesn't try in school. He's very bright and he obviously could do the work if he'd try."

"Ever since he was a little boy, he'd sit in class and not listen or turn in assignments. Put him in front of a video game or on a football field and he was brilliant!"

This type of conversation continued for a few minutes, and then the counselor turned to Jason and asked, "Jason, what do you think of your parents' opinions?"

"They're so stupid!" Jason answered sullenly. "Everybody expects me to be a neurosurgeon. Can't they get it through their heads that I'm not smart like they think I am? Why don't they just get off my back?"

Over several sessions, a story unfolded of gradual human depletion. Jason, it turned out, had already gathered a long history of failure. From nursery school onward, his average-level work had never satisfied his parents. While Jason truly was not able to pull off all honors grades, his parents' vicarious dreams demanded that he achieve at the top of the class. Gradually, he learned to believe in himself less and less. Since he believed that his parents' dream for his life was the right one, and that he could not live up to that dream, Jason began to withdraw. Finally, he stopped trying altogether, began skipping classes, and not completing assignments. His parents' dream was undermining his sense of his own competence and value.

DREAM FACTORS

It would be wonderful if, at this point, we could write a simple list of *Factors For Workable and Fulfilling Dreams*. If this were possible, our book would be much shorter. In reality, there are a lot of reasons why dreams do or do not work. Any person's life-dream may have a combination of these positive and negative factors and the factors in any dream may overlap and complement or detract from each other. For example, a system may have plenty of resources to accomplish great dreams, but all those resources may be stymied by a strong systemic rigidity that prevents creativity.

When the overall negativity level is high enough, the person has to work so hard trying to sustain the dream, that the human spirit becomes depleted. It is important to assess dreams, weighing their positive and negative factors. The weight of each factor will vary from person to person. To steal a saying from another story, while one person might find that his dream has too many negative factors to sustain it, another might say, "It ain't heavy; it's my dream." While one person will not want to test a dream until it has reached his or her standard of perfection, another will step boldly forth with a dream that is far from perfect, thinking, "I can work on this along the way."

Because of individual differences, no one can tell another person the answers to life's dream questions. This is a quest which each of us must undertake for ourselves. However, listed below are some questions which may support you in that quest.

- What are some things a dream must hold for me to consider it satisfying?
- How many negativity factors (obstacles) am I willing to live with? How much energy do I have to work around obstacles?
- What would constitute success for me?
- What would I experience as failure?
- Who else shares my dream? How much weight do I place on their part in it?
- Who is (are) responsible for this dream happening?
- Can my dream be revised? How much? In what areas?
- What am I willing to contribute to carry out revisions?
- How does my dream fit into the system (organization) at this time? Might there be a better time for my dream to fit into the system?
- What might I do/think/feel that would enhance my satisfaction with my professional dream?

THE GET-AWAY HELPING FACTOR

Often, the possibility factor of dreams is contingent upon the ability of the dreamer to hold the reins on his or her own caregiving. While it may not be possible to reform a whole educational system, it may be completely realistic to say, "I will be the best teacher I can for the children who come into my classroom, and when they leave my care, I will pass them on to their next teacher." In a similar way, the oncologist who realizes that even with her best efforts many patients will die, can still derive satisfaction from her willingness and ability to offer hope for the best possible life quality for as long as those patients live.

No matter how competent the surgeon, some patients will die. Even in the midst of therapy, people commit suicide. The best teacher cannot always overcome environmental and family impediments to a child's ability to learn. Even the greatest prophets of history could not persuade most people to lead holy lives.

Many—perhaps most—people entering caregiving professions do so out of a dream to help others. This is a wonderful and rewarding dream, both for the caregiver and for the world. Often, however, the dream is so exciting, it begins to take over more and more aspects of our lives, and we end up wanting to COMPLETELY help ALL others. The dream *gets away* on us and takes us with it. Those of us who have been programmed as children and through our professional training to reach out to others and ignore our own needs are especially vulnerable to the get-away factor, because it may be quite a while before we even notice that we are no longer holding the reins. The dream is steering itself! Instead of being the drivers, we have become the servants of the dream. This attitude, in its moderate version, leads to harried professionals with endless to-do lists. It becomes intolerable as it becomes accompanied by a sense of defeat and an assault on the spirit with thoughts like, "I can never be enough."

Check out the exercise below to help you discern if you have a weighty *Hooked On Helping Factor* in your dream.

Read the following questions and place yourself on a 10-point scale, where 1 is *almost never/not at all* and 10 is almost *always/almost completely.*

- (1 2 3 4 5 6 7 8 9 10)   I have a hard time saying "no" when someone asks for help.

- (1 2 3 4 5 6 7 8 9 10)   I often see help I can give to people even when they, themselves, have not seen what they need.

• (1 2 3 4 5 6 7 8 9 10)   I put other people's needs before my own.

• (1 2 3 4 5 6 7 8 9 10)   I feel guilty or selfish when I play or rest.

• (1 2 3 4 5 6 7 8 9 10)   I get my needs met by helping others.

• (1 2 3 4 5 6 7 8 9 10)   If I am tired and another person needs help, I'll put aside my fatigue and respond.

• (1 2 3 4 5 6 7 8 9 10)   I feel awful when I see a painful situation in which I am powerless to change.

• (1 2 3 4 5 6 7 8 9 10)   I worry a lot about other people.

• (1 2 3 4 5 6 7 8 9 10)   I underestimate the time it takes to make an intervention or complete a project.

• (1 2 3 4 5 6 7 8 9 10)   I forget that I, too, can get the common cold.

When you have tallied your score for the questions above, only you can decide if your level is too high or even toxic. We suggest that you copy this list and display it in a prominent place, perhaps your bathroom mirror or desktop.

THE OMNIPOTENCE AND OMNISCIENCE FACTORS

On the day she was ordained, Elizabeth thought that she could not be happier. Her lifelong goal had been accomplished. She was assigned to a mid-size church in a major city. She knew that she was well-prepared to minister and to share God's love with others. She saw herself as appointed by God to share the message of love.

By the time she had been in ministry for five years, Elizabeth was thoroughly disillusioned. Everyone, from her pastoral superiors to the youngest members of the congregation, seemed to have expectations for her. She spent most of her time running around trying to provide what other people wanted, with gritting teeth and a smile on her face. Elizabeth did not want to say, "No," to anyone. She did not want to force any confrontations. She just wanted everyone to be happy. In the process, she had lost her sense of herself and of who she was in ministry. In trying to be god-like, she had lost her own personhood.

Many caregivers set themselves up with the impossible tasks of omnipotence and omniscience. A teacher may not be willing to admit that he doesn't know all the answers. In doing so, he nurtures in his students an attitude that one should only attempt tasks at which one is sure to succeed. In fact, having had, himself, parents and teachers with that attitude may be the reason why a teacher cannot accept that he does not need to know all the answers.

A physician may believe that she cannot fail or make a mistaken diagnosis. Then the unforgivable happens—a patient questions the physician's judgment—another professional disagrees with the physician's diagnosis—a patient has the temerity to die—and this physician finds herself questioning her own value and seeing herself as a failure. She forgets that it is humanly impossible to be right all the time.

In helping professions, this attitude is often strengthened because society expects omnipotence and omniscience. Professional caregivers become legally liable for human limitations. A therapist who was being sued because a client in his care committed suicide said, "This is a nightmare I've had ever since my first year in grad school. Now it's coming true. This man came to me in a deep depression. I believe I gave him excellent care. He died anyway. Now, I'm being held responsible. I lie awake at night wondering how I could have better cared for him!"

We need to give ourselves permission to make mistakes, to learn and grow, and to try risky ventures. We need the ability to change plans in midstream when new information surfaces. Sometimes accepting that we do not always need to *know everything* can help us find courage to attempt the very difficult tasks of life. Taking away this expectation is like taking away fences that have kept us away from a full life. With the fences gone, we are able to allow in the insights and gifts of others. We find that we do not need to solve the world's problems by ourselves. As we allow ourselves to be less omniscient and omnipotent, we invite others to think, create, and do.

Allowing ourselves to be human can be a very freeing sensation. Not long ago, those of us who were trained to be therapists, were trained to reflect none of our humanity, to project the "blank screen" image to the client. More recently, we have been listening to the clients who tell us that it is in ethically using our own personhood, and not setting aside our own struggles, that we become more effective therapists. Together, the therapist and the client construct a new sense of life and reality which is useful as the client interacts with his world. In her book *Partners in Healing; Redistributing Power in the Counselor-Client Relationship,* Barbara Friedman, Ph.D. offers excellent and pragmatic guidelines for the development of this relational reality between caregivers and those for whom we care [2].

THE SYSTEMIC FACTOR

Even the most realistic dream can only thrive in a system which can nurture it. In our contemporary world, a strange dichotomy has arisen. On the one hand, books on organizational effectiveness advise managers to develop systems with room for creative employees to maneuver and contribute, and which also honor the needs of the employee's personal life. On the other hand, budget restraints have often forced managers to tighten up in all these areas. This can be confusing to people at all levels in the system.

Many caregivers' dreams are based upon notions of systems which do not exist. One of the clear findings of the Alberta study is that teachers must function within far-from-ideal systems. They begin their careers steeped in ideals which will enable them to help children, to make a difference in the world. Before long, they realize that educational systems are bogged down for many reasons, not the least of which are politics and bureaucracies. This discrepancy between the ideal and reality causes great stress. Similarly, when intensive care nurses at a major hospital were surveyed, they shared that a major stress on their lives was the discrepancy between their ideal of a hospital which truly responded to patient needs, and the reality of a hospital based on a profit motive and controlled by insurance regulations set by faceless individuals who never saw the patients.

One way individuals and the systems which employ them often clash is over ethical issues. The television show *Chicago Hope* often shows this clash. There are idealistic physicians and nurses and an idealistic lawyer, all wanting to have the hospital represent their personal values. The lawyer's responsibility is to make the hospital look good, no matter what. Sometimes, this mandate clashes with his respect and friendship for the medical personnel and their agendas. The physicians' Hippocratic Oath means that they must place the patient's needs above those of the hospital or staff. However, there are often differing interpretations of the phrase "doing only good" for the patient.

Then there are the values of the larger society in which the hospital functions, which may or may not support the values of the caregivers.

Intensive care nurses repeatedly raise ethical questions. "How much sedation can we give a dying patient?" "How do I lovingly care for the drunk whose car hit the woman in the next bed who will likely die?" "What should my response be to the convicted murderer who is brought from prison for open heart surgery at the taxpayers' expense?" "Which patients are more worthy of organ transplants when there is only one organ and three dying patients?"

A nurse said, "I speak for many of my colleagues when I say we're scared. We're all worried that someone in our care might die because we are too short-staffed to give the kind of nursing care that we are trained to do."

Many systems do not provide forums to address these issues. Others care about the angst of the employees, but feel that for their own reasons (often financial), they cannot cooperate with the caregivers' needs.

Budget constraints are systemic factors which often feed feelings of frustration. Cutbacks have left less caregivers hustling to care for more people with fewer resources. Disillusionment is common. A teacher said, "The County has a huge budget deficit because of unexpected repairs to the stadium for professional baseball and football. Now they are suggesting they'll make that up by taking it out of the budgets for education and police protection!"

THE TIMING FACTORS

Everyone has heard it said of certain individuals, "She is ahead of her time." There will always be people whose dreams do not fit into the reality of their times. Many of them are visionaries, who dream of something which will actually come to pass, but not at the time they plan for it to happen. Others are just impatient folks, who are unable or unwilling to patiently plant and nurture seeds to bring their dreams to fruition. Whatever the reason, these folks are out of sync with reality, and experience great frustration because their plans and work do not bear fruit.

David, a middle-aged pastor, sat with his head in his hands and said, "I can't understand why nothing works. I want this parish to be like the early church—with everyone supporting each other; women and men in collaborative community. I want them to stand up for their faith and to prioritize parish activities on their schedules. I can't build it alone. But they are so apathetic! How do I motivate them?"

David was dreaming of a church without all the historical baggage of his contemporary parish. He was out of sync with the reality of the time.

Peg is a contemporary police officer. She has an abundance of modern scientific equipment and training. A major aspect of her training has been in public relations and she spends much of her time in community work, which her superiors believe pays off in decreased violence and crime. However, whenever she visits her father and grandfather, who live together and who are both retired police officers, she is teased and scolded. "Why can't you do real police work? We used to spend our time catching bad guys, not playing with kids." She returns to work confused and frustrated that perhaps she is not living out the family tradition. It takes her a couple of days to return to a sense of the rightness of her professional life.

Another way the timing factor can impact dreams is by accepting that we are sometimes too old to accomplish certain life goals. A woman in her fifties shared, "I'd love to go to college and learn to be a teacher. But I'm too old to start over." A teacher about the same age said, "I'm not enjoying what I do, but I'm too old to learn another job."

Many of us have stereotypes about aging. Jack Canfield and Mark Hansen remind us, with the story of Walt Jones, that age need not be limiting [3]. At eighty-seven years old, after the death of his wife of fifty-two years, Walt bought a motor home and toured over forty states, married again at 104 and made a thirty-year investment at 108. Grandma Moses never painted as a young woman. We are entering a new era, when ageism simply is not acceptable. You would not get away professionally with prejudice against seniors; apply the same standards to judging yourself. Just because your hair has turned gray there is no reason not to follow your dream. Your age and wisdom, in fact, may be an asset in new endeavors.

THE SIZE AND FUNDING FACTORS

Together with the timing factor, the size and funding factors are often the basic reasons why dreams based in systems often do not work.

Grandiose dreams, which are larger than the corporate funding base, cannot succeed. Funding may be in monetary currency, or in available talent or energy. Whatever the need, if the reality does not match the expectation, then frustration, stress, and failure will occur.

Francis had a dream. He cherished the dream all through college, medical school, and residency, and then he set about to make it happen. He wanted to establish a free clinic in the inner city, funded by the for-profit clinics and hospitals of the area. His clinic would care for children and pregnant women, treat addictions, teach nutrition, and generally nurture the bodies and psyches of the residents of the inner city.

Francis found a building which he thought was perfect. He persuaded the owner to cut the rent. He canvassed for donations of equipment and medications. He then began to persuade his colleagues to donate time at the clinic. He did this by showing them all the groundwork he had laid, believing that when they saw the facility and statistics for donations promised, they would all be eager to sign up on his schedule to volunteer.

However, Francis had not realized that most of the medical personnel in his area were already very busy with work, families, and service involvements of their own choosing. They were already spread as thinly as possible. Only a few were interested in Francis' dream, and nobody was willing to invest deeply. Somehow, Francis had been able to lay the financial groundwork for making his dream come true, but he could not find the necessary personnel or talent. So Francis worked at the clinic himself.

Because this was his own dream and he was running it, Francis was able to sustain the clinic for over five years. Eventually, however, he grew disillusioned and was having chronic stomach problems and back pain. He had to close the clinic and allow himself time to heal and develop another dream for helping the poor.

When Francis could no longer keep his clinic open, people were sad, and blamed the happening on fatigue. That factor, however, was far less important than the disillusionment Francis had experienced, and he left the city with deep bitterness.

Workable dreams take into account factors of funding, both with labor and with finances. Making a dream realistic sometimes means cutting back, setting priorities, and developing a plan with workable phases—recognizing that the accomplishment of any one phase is both a success in itself *and* a stepping-stone to the next phase.

THE FLEXIBILITY FACTOR

How many times have you heard the expression "I need more space!" The language of space is often associated with descriptions of dreams and projects. "We are expanding." "Our capital is shrinking." Without flexibility, there is very little space to maneuver—emotionally, intellectually, or practically—for change. Anyone who has built a successful dream will tell us how important maneuvering is!

Maneuvering is not manipulating in its negative sense. It is the ability to try things and see if they work and then restructure plans and goals around those results. Dreams require flexible plans. As its plan comes strongly up against the rigid factors of life, a flexible dream has the ability to gently conform to those structures, or to slide around them. It is not broken by them.

To catch a fish, you need a flexible pole and line. To ski down a mountain, you need flexible skis. In an earthquake, it is the less flexible structures that tumble apart. In a strong wind, the flexible willow will bend and survive, while the rigid fir may lose its head.

What makes a dream flexible? Often, it is a belief in the creativity of the dreamer—knowing that Plan B is always waiting if Plan A doesn't work.

The enemy of flexibility is often fear. If people do not feel control over their environment, they develop rigid structures. In these rigid structures, dreams cannot flourish.

Think of someone you feel is rigid. If you could see behind this person's day-to-day persona, what fear might you identify? Fear of losing control? Fear of sharing the glory? Fear of doing something less than perfectly? Fear of failure?

Can you think of a rigid policy in your organization that limits creativity? How do such policies make it more difficult to live out dreams? Can you identify the fear behind the policy? Is the policy, in fact, actually working for those who set it, or does it inhibit even their dreams from developing? If you were to change this policy, what would you suggest? How might you help those who set policies to overcome their fears? Is there an antidote to fear in your organization?

For many people, the thing which creates the most fear is the belief that they need to succeed in everything on the first try—and that if they do not do it better than anyone else, they are failures. Perfectionism is a killer of dreams!

Flexibility demands courage—courage to take risks, believing that we need not succeed the first time. We need to be able to know that our dreams may not work at all, but that there is nobility and grace in the journey. Like Don Quixote, the quest needs to thrill us enough so we will risk failure and keep trying.

One of the ways dreams lose flexibility is through the development of bureaucracies around the dreams themselves. Bureaucracies often begin as attempts to bring order to large systems. Unfortunately, bureaucracies themselves have a strong get-away potential and sometimes they take over, with the bureaucracy eventually driving and defining the system. When this happens, dreams may be smothered and aspirations limited.

Social workers, who enter their field with dreams of service, often find that they may spend as little as 30 percent of their time in direct service, and the remaining time, nurturing the bureaucracy. It may have been a social worker who first coined the song "Here we go 'round the referral tree, the referral tree, the referral tree. . . ." People who need assistance find themselves standing in line and feeling demeaned. In attempting to improve the situation, the bureaucracy tries to become more efficient, but actually grows larger and larger, and places the receiver farther and farther from service, and the caregiver farther and farther from those whom he cares for. For many caregivers in such systems, the dream becomes mutated and the goal becomes one of climbing within the system, rather than of rendering direct care.

The greater the gap between the mission of the organization and the ability to deliver service, the greater the chance that dedicated caregivers will begin to feel a vague ache inside. They haven't yet identified their dilemma, but the voices of their spirit have been so muffled they may no longer hear them. Many of their colleagues seem to do fine with the system. They begin to doubt their own experiences. Are they the only ones who think the system is not working?

One aspect of flexibility is in knowing when to withdraw one's dream from an existing structure and take it elsewhere, where it can grow to fruition. Sometimes, a person does this with his relationship dream, leaving a marriage that does not work and seeking something more fulfilling. Just as often, as caregivers, we need to assess whether the structures within which we have implanted our professional dreams can sustain and give life to those visions, or whether we need to look for alternative structures. People who bang their heads against brick walls seldom break through. More often, they end up with flat heads!

Making the decision to remove one's personal investments from a system, however, is often not easy. If we had only the professional dream to consider, if alternative jobs were plentiful, such decisions would be simple. One could move from job to job, looking for a perfect fit.

For several reasons, it is important that such decisions be carefully considered. In frustration, we tend to make hasty decisions, often "throwing the baby out with the bath water." It is important to carefully assess the whole situation. Often, at the moment when we think our dream is dying, we can perform a miracle of resuscitation, finding that the dream is more vital than it had seemed.

When we were children, we were amazed at the early Walt Disney films showing a flower opening and closing. How much more meaningful that was than a simple photograph of a rose or a daisy! Dreams, too, need to have movement and change built in. A dream that is simply a snapshot frozen in time will not have the ability to flow with a changing reality.

Ronna and Alan, both entering marriage for a second time, wrote their wedding vows with the realization that their dream needed flexibility. Included in the vows were the following:

- I will appreciate your strengths and not ask you to be like me.
- I will cherish your uniqueness and encourage your growth.
- I will strive to understand our differences, seeing them as gifts, not problems. I will request, not demand change.
- I will have a dream and not ask you to provide me with purpose. I will negotiate shared goals and support you in your dreams.
- I will give our relationship overall priority and join you in a vigil to protect us from the clutter of life.

• I will negotiate times and commitments that temporarily unbalance our lives.

Think of an important relationship in your life. Do the ways in which you have been living your dreams in that relationship have flexibility factors built in? What might you do to improve the situation?

THE DEPTH AND WIDTH FACTOR

Shallow dreams expect everyone involved to conform to the dreamer's agenda and needs. Dreams that are deep and wide often have space for input from many sources and an excitement for growing together. Learning to recognize the line between overly narrow or shallow, and too wide or deep, is one of the tasks of successful dreamers.

Often, we confuse narrowness with reality. "I need to be realistic about my dreams," we say. "There's no use spending time and energy on a dream that can't work." Unfortunately, the "reality" we embrace is often defined by other people. One of the most difficult tasks of dreamcrafting is deciding what is really possible, given the existing environment and resources. The *Serenity Prayer* so beloved by 12-steppers could offer guidelines for dreamers: *God grant me the serenity to accept the things I cannot change; the courage to change the things I can; and the wisdom to know the difference.*

For every dream, there is a line between rigid narrowness and overblown grandiosity, between being realistic and inappropriately limiting our vision. Finding that line may be the most difficult part of crafting a dream that works. It may involve trying things out to see what will work, much like a beginning swimmer will gradually enter the water, checking to be sure he will not drop off beyond his depth. Even in this testing and planning stage, flexibility, the ability to fail and try again, is vitally important.

Like all the factors described here, the depth and width factors must be integrated with the other factors. Assessing available resources and funding, examining the levels of energy and courage, and a healthy awareness of the strengths and limitations of pertaining systems are all necessary before one can decide if a dream is as deep and wide as it needs to be, or if it is so deep and wide that it cannot work.

If Francis, when he wanted to reach out to the poor, had decided to open his own office to these patients for two hours a day, he may have been able to sustain and find great satisfaction from his dream. But he tried to address too broad a picture with too few resources.

One problem is that we seldom take time for assessment, but are carried away by the dreams without careful planning. It takes courage to say, "I am going to carefully assess whether this dream has a chance to work, or whether I need to find another dream which can work." Who wants to learn that a dream can't work? Because we shy away from this possibility, we sometimes skip the appropriate assessment phase of dreaming.

THE AUTHENTICITY FACTOR

Inauthentic dreams—dreams from other people which do not naturally live within our souls, but which, like hermit crabs, have taken over the homes of our authentic dreams—will surely pull us toward burnout. There is no way a person can find life fulfillment from another person's dream. It just is not possible.

This factor is perhaps the major one in determining burnout. How can one feel whole when the soulplace is being inhabited by someone else's dreams? This is what happened to Jason, the high school student who was burning out and withdrawing before even reaching adulthood. His parents' dreams were toxic to him. Well-meant and loving, but absolutely wrong for Jason, these dreams had stolen his sense of his own goodness and competence, until he had escaped by refraining from even trying to succeed.

Many other people do not burn out as quickly as Jason. Instead, they invest years and years of their lives into education and professional development in careers which belong to the dreams of their parents or other mentors. Then one day, they either become ill or lose interest in their work. Sometimes, they actually begin to dislike their work. Then, they are caught in the quandary that they want something, but feel too old to make changes. Sometimes, this also happens in marriages, where one or both partners are unhappy but neither can move to end the relationship and reinvest in lives which would be more meaningful.

THE FOCUS FACTOR

A key ingredient to making a dream work is the dreamer's ability to focus attention and resources in accomplishing it. This may seem obvious but it is a factor which many people do not consider. Over half of freshman university students drop out. Only 15 to 20 percent of Ph.D. students make it to graduation. Thousands of small businesses go broke every week. Donna, who is in private practice, often meets colleagues who are complaining that their practices are not growing. When asked about their efforts, it is clear that many of these people are ill prepared to work at business development and are floundering under an illusion that clients and patients will just come to them. In some cases, they are prepared to work only certain hours, when the "therapist down the road" will see clients in the evening or on weekends.

We could call this sort of dream the *undisciplined dream.* Planning and/or execution may lack focused energy and patience. As authors, we realize that writing a book does not prove that we know any more about a subject than our colleagues. It does, however, show that we have learned to discipline ourselves to set aside the time for research and writing, to wait for that wonderful moment when a publisher shows interest, and to complete tedious editorial work. Projects like this, creating something new or different from what has existed before, can take the dreamer on a roller coaster ride. These dreams only come to fruition if the dreamer is disciplined and believes strongly in the dream.

There is nothing wrong with those people who are not able or willing to focus time and attention on their dream in meaningful ways. They do, however, face the hurt and puzzlement of seeing their glowing dream turn into a daydream—a bittersweet "if only." There is nothing wrong with assessing the discipline that will be needed and deciding that this dream is not what you want. The problems arise when people decide they want a dream but neglect to consider what that dream will cost.

Do you have a dream? Are having a problem getting focused? Is this dream, in fact, authentically your own or has it been adopted from someone else? Are you having a problem defining the scope or demands of the dream? If so, is there someone who could help you with this process? How might you invite that person into your dream and ask for his or her support and guidance?

THE GENDER FACTOR

Society has made strides toward becoming gender-equal. It has a long way to go. In nearly every caring profession, there is an inequality in numbers—more men or more women. The professions where the pay is higher have more men. Even today, high school boys are discouraged from becoming nurses and girls are often told, "It takes a lot of time and energy to become a doctor. Are you sure you want to make that commitment when you'll be wanting to marry and have children?" Pastoral caregivers are predominantly men. Many faith groups still will not ordain women and in those which do, there are less opportunities for women to assume highly-influential leadership positions. Young men who want to teach small children are often viewed with suspicion.

It takes strong conviction to cling to a dream when those we respect are saying it will not work. One of the problems is that for those in the less-common gender of our professions, there are few role models. Women who become physicians tell us that they struggle to understand how to be feminine and still compete in a predominantly masculine atmosphere. Fortunately for the world, there have been enough women who passionately believed in their dreams, and the inequities are becoming fewer. Medical schools and many professional training programs, however, still work with predominantly masculine learning styles.

DREAMS THAT GIVE LIFE

For every dream that cannot work, there are many others which can and do come to fruition, providing fulfillment and joy to the dreamers and hope to the world. Throughout history, there have been mighty dreamcrafters. Martin Luther King, Jr. and John F. Kennedy, were ordinary, flawed human beings, whose ability to dream could excite not only a nation, but the whole world, causing their dreams to take on lives of their own and come to fruition long after the original dreamers had died. Mother Theresa, a simple nun, dreamed of a safe and dignified place for some "street people" in Calcutta to die, and today her vision of caring has spread worldwide.

These sorts of dreams could be considered impossible, like Don Quixote tilting at windmills. Instead, they somehow energize the world and, like magnets, attract people and resources. The Statue of Liberty, brought to New York from France and replicated in Tienanmen Square, has been built again in Canada on the campus of the University of British Columbia, to symbolize efforts for Chinese democracy. In World Wars I and II, soldiers from all over the world converged upon European countries to defend the concept of liberty. The United Nations is today's reality because of the dream of a few people over half a century ago. These dreams have all been bigger than the original dreamers.

Most caregivers have dreams of a better world—a world where illiteracy, sickness, poverty, and bigotry will cease to exist. These dreams are also larger than the original dreamers. If the dream is, in fact, the dreamer's own, and if the institutions within which the dreams are implanted have the ability to sustain the dreamers' needs, then, for at least some people, the world becomes a finer place to live. Once in a while, a dream is so sturdy and the dreamer so strong, that the dream survives intact through great oppression and persecution. Nelson Mandela, imprisoned for twenty-seven years by South Africa's apartheid government, now sits as president of the same country which seemed to be rejecting his dream. In reality, even though he was isolated and gagged from speaking, his voice was taken up by others who shared his dream. His very persecution became part of the energy that brought his vision to reality.

Passion and hope are as necessary to growing dreams as yeast is to rising bread. Passionate hope and hopeful passion join to flavor the dream reality and give spice to the necessary patience and flexibility.

Dreams that give life are dreams that give. They are not ego-driven. In Edmonton, Canada, two dreams are coming to fruition. West Edmonton Mall is an amazing complex of shops, services, and entertainment that draws tourists from all over North America. In West Edmonton Mall, for a fee, people can bask in the "sun" on a sandy "beach" when the temperature outside is cold enough to freeze unexposed flesh in five minutes. For a price, one can buy just about anything one desires. For a price, one can dine in luxury or ride a roller coaster as fast and high as any in the world. And at the end of a day at West Edmonton Mall, customers leave with empty wallets and a sense that the acquisition of material things, or the experience of bungy jumping from a crane into a wave pool, has fulfilled their hunger to feel alive. West Edmonton Mall has become the shopping hub for northern Alberta. Sounds good, doesn't it? But on the other side of the coin, what has its convenience and grandiosity done to hundreds of other small businesses? Unable to compete, how many of these shops and services are now closed, the buildings which housed them blindly facing the streets with empty, dark windows? Is this a life-giving project? The answer is not simple.

Also in Edmonton, another dream has been growing slowly, with great persistence, passion, and courage. On a quiet city street on the campus of the University of Alberta, an unusable house was repaired by volunteer labor and donations, transformed into a home for The Hope Foundation, a symbol of courage and hope. The primary objective and vision of this foundation is to understand this thing we call *hope* and to apply it in practical ways. What if we could learn enough about *hope* to become as intentional about it as we are about our dental hygiene? Grants are funding the salaries of a few professionals. Local business people are joining in the vision. Partnership is an essential component of the vision for a hopeful future. The dream is giving life to many and is growing, as more and more dreamers are inspired to join. As with many dreams, much depends on financial funding. In the meantime, *making a difference* is already happening. The heart of the dream is alive. What might happen if cities wanted to be known as places of *hope,* if there was a *Hope Street* in the heart of a city? That's a life-giving dream.

Life-giving dreams come forth from spirit, from the soul of the dreamer. The voice of one's soul is the articulation of the dream and gives it life. People throughout time have understood the importance of spirit. Thousands of years ago, trying to explain how humankind came to be, an author wrote, in the creation story from Genesis, that through His Spirit, Yahweh breathed life into humanity and into all of creation [4].

Spirit is what gets us out of bed the morning after a disappointing day. It energizes us to make one more phone call after a day of rejection, to study those extra hours for the difficult exam, and to wait patiently until the frightened client or patient is ready to accept appropriate treatment. It listens carefully to the confused student, and in the listening, communicates empathy and encouragement.

The spirit's voice in a caregiver's dream will passionately reach out to the spirits of hurting or needy people. Spirits interconnect gently and empowerment begins. The wounded spirit of the other becomes aware of the dream and begins to find hope. It replenishes itself at the well of the passionate dream spirit.

I (Donna) was a patient in a large university hospital. Frightened and in acute pain, I could find no source of strength. Staff persons hurried from room to room. Voices laughed in the hallway. The radio of another patient filled the room with rock music. Outside, a huge jack hammer broke away at the next building. And I lay scarcely able to breathe, unable to call out, tears streaming down my face. A group of student nurses stood outside the door and one woman looked in. She quickly sent the younger women away and moved to my bedside, lowered the bedside bars, and sat down. Reaching out, she gently raised my upper body and cradled it in her arms. Speaking softly and reassuringly, she soothed away my fears. Suddenly I could breathe with less pain. The room seemed brighter. I found hope. My spirit was revived.

That nurse stayed with me for about fifteen minutes. Her intervention meant more to my recovery than all the medical treatments combined. She gave me back the will to fight off the infection. At least twenty years later, I remember her and I can remember no one else from that three-week hospital stay.

My body could not heal without one nurse's personal touch. Dreams which give life demand action by the participants. *Cities of Hope* will not grow without passionate commitment and action from many people. Without involvement, a dream is empty. We need to fill our dreams with our actions. Our actions make our passion and our hope a reality.

The world needs dreams and dream-bearers. Without dreamers, nothing could happen. The Dead Sea is dead because water can only enter it. There is no outlet for the water to flow away. It can only evaporate, leaving behind a sea that is stagnant. Our dreams provide the movement for life and keep life from becoming stagnant and toxic. If we allow our dreams to stop flowing, they will become stagnant like the Dead Sea. Stagnant dreams, like stagnant water, are toxic and lead to a life which feels less and less fulfilling, and eventually lead to burnout.

QUESTIONS FOR REFLECTION: EXAMINING MY DREAM

1. Who do I recognize as dream-bearers for our society?
2. Who is or has been a dream-bearer who inspired me personally? What parts of that person's vision have I adopted? What elements have I personally added to the dream?
3. What is the heart of my dream? Does it emanate from my soul, my spirit? Or is it inspired externally, by other people's values or by wishes for material wealth?
4. Are there any factors which deplete my dream's energy and limit its possibilities?
5. What factors of my dream are life giving—to me?—to other people?
6. If I had a large sum of money, would my dream change? How?
7. Am I listening to the voice of my dream, or locking it away so it cannot call to me?

REFERENCES

1. E. Doan, *Speakers Sourcebook,* Zondervan Corporation, Grand Rapids, Michigan, 1960.
2. B. Friedman, *Partners in Healing; Redistributing Power in the Counselor-Client Relationship,* Resource Publications, Inc., San Jose, California, 1992.
3. J. Canfield and M. Hansen, *Chicken Soup For The Soul; 101 Stories to Open the Heart and Rekindle the Spirit,* Health Communications, Inc., Deerfield Beach, Florida, 1993.
4. Genesis 2:7.

CHAPTER 5

The Professional Caregiver Dream

> Everybody has a sort of holiness inside himself. Why? We don't know why, but everybody has. We have no God outside. We have some sort of God inside. We don't know how it works or its origins but I think it's generations and generations of hope and despair and prayer and what the church of today has to do is to tell people of this holiness and to educate everybody to come into intuitive contact with that part soon.
>
> *Ingmar Bergman; in discussion*
> *following the movie* Winter Light

When we began to tell people that we wanted to write this book based on the results of the Alberta teacher's study, we heard the same comment from several people, "It sounds as if these are insights for anyone with a job. Why are you centering your book on the experience of caregivers?" This question led us to examine our concept of who a caregiver really is. Is there actually a different frame of mind, a life stance which differs between the physician and the architect, the teacher and the engineer, the priest and the greengrocer? Do those in the caregiving professions share some common attitudes which support or hinder their healthy professional lives?

We think so. This is not to say that there are not caring mechanics or compassionate accountants. The person who chooses an overtly caregiving profession, however, may hear a different call. Articulating this essence, this unique voice which emanates from the soul of the caregiver, demanded our contemplation and discussion, and comprises the contents of this chapter.

Who are we who choose to spend our lives helping others find abundant life? Who are our models? How are we different from other professionals—from the artist or the scientist? Why do we choose caregiving professions? What difference is there between a professional caregiver and a non-professional one? The questions never end.

WHO AM I?

As we wrote in Chapter 2, having a sense of who one is, of one's unique personhood and place in the world, is vital to healthy living. One does not need to spend much time around caregivers to realize that many of us get an inordinate amount of our self-identity from the work we do. We do not have *jobs*. We *hold positions* and have *careers*. We teach essential life skills and expand the minds of youth. We mend broken bones and broken lives. We pick up hurting people from the edges of life, brush them off, bandage their hurts, and educate them so life won't knock them down again.

We are the helper folk who make the world less scary. Often, when and if we cannot accomplish these things, we hold ourselves responsible. We care more and work harder than before, and in doing this, we feel less inadequate.

Teachers in the Alberta study expressed that the level of energy they believed was required for professional life left none for personal pursuits.

> I think, especially as primary teachers, we feel so driven to have every child be successful. We spend so much time on self-esteem for the children and not for ourselves . . .

> Well, I always used whatever time was left over after everybody else's needs were met and this servitude that teachers have . . . you just, if you have Friday nights, throw yourself on the couch and you're asleep in five minutes. But that's your time. My husband would pick me up from school and I would be asleep in the car before we got home. . . . [1, pp. 14-15].

There are those people who would call us "unhealthy." They use words like *co-dependent* and *needing to be needed*. The authors prefer not to think of ourselves or of other helping people in that way. Why should we pathologize a perfectly normal condition? We believe that most people who become caregivers are just warm, caring individuals who have been blessed with an abundance of sensitivity and concern for others, combined with certain kinds of talent. It is true that many of us come from families with poor relational skills. But so do many farmers and pharmacists, bus drivers, and biochemists. In fact, a great many people, perhaps most, in all walks of life were born into less-than-perfect families. It is also true that many of us are oldest children, who learned to care for our younger siblings out of necessity. But many of us are also youngest, middle, and only children. We come from all sorts of families and belong to all races and religions. There is no simple profile of a caregiver. Some of us are extra needy for affirmation and affection, while others feel only a healthy need for feedback from those whose lives are touched by our care.

There are, however, some common strands to our profiles. A large component of self-identity is invested in the professions to which we belong. We think of ourselves as teachers, nurses, physicians, therapists, and ministers. We fight fires, save lives and protect the innocent. We are proud of what we do and how well we do it, and we derive a large part of our understanding of who we are from that pride.

Think about it. If a stranger asked you who you were, would you say, "My name is George Smith and I am married to Martha and have three children. I enjoy baseball and belong to First Presbyterian Church. I'm rather moody and have a fierce temper. I'm generous and kind. Oh yes—and I'm a cardiac surgeon." Or would the way you shared the parameters of your life begin with, "My name is Dr. George Smith and I'm a cardiac surgeon. . . ."

WHO DO I CARE FOR?

Another trait many caregivers have in common is that we will reach out to others but pay little attention to our own needs.

We will sacrifice ourselves on the "altar of caring." Those of us whose professions demand that we place ourselves in physical danger for the good of others are usually aware of this dynamic. But the rest of us tend to do the same thing in more subtle ways.

Often, we have very little sense of ourselves outside our professional lives, and do not notice the inner voices that tell us to rest or recreate. In this, again, we are not unique. Many people who are not caregivers have a very poor sense of their own personhood. Perhaps the difference is that when we caregivers lack a strong sense of self, we have found a unique way to fill the empty places within. Rather than pursuing money or collecting achievements, we fill these gaping holes with concern for others. Thus we come to see ourselves as "people who care for others." Our caregiving becomes our identity.

WHAT PART DOES MY SENSE OF MYSELF AS A PROFESSIONAL PLAY IN MY SELF-IMAGE?

There are many people from all walks of life who spend a lot of time caring for others, but who never become professional caregivers. Those of us who do usually have a strong wish to do things well. We are willing to spend many years and a great deal of money and energy learning how to give care the professional way. It is important to us that we carry the proper credentials to establish our credibility as professional caregivers. We commit ourselves to the codes of ethics of our professions and believe that we have the ability to make a difference.

As we become people who identify with the words *professional caregiver* as self-descriptive, we further lose sight of other aspects of who we are. After a while, our caregiver dreams may completely take over our self-images. That is when our lives become unbalanced and externalized.

LISTENING TO THE VOICE OF MY SOUL

This unbalancing happens more easily and quickly for people who truly have very little sense of who they are as persons. *To be healthy, a sense of unique personhood must precede the caregiver identity.* We call this sense of uniqueness the *voice of the soul.* Unfortunately, for many—perhaps most—people, the childhood environment provides very few experiences for self-definition and a multitude of experiences for learning to define ourselves as others would have us be. This leaves that vacant soul space waiting for some sense of identity to fill it. These people quickly and easily define themselves by their professional identities. Since they usually have a very minimal sense of themselves, it is also usually the case that their professional aspirations arose from the voices and expectations of other people. Since the self-image implanted within the soul space is not authentic to the individual, there arises a strong and consistent dissonance within the person's very being.

Developmentally, even if we pay very little attention to our souls' needs, as we grow older the authentic voices of our souls tend to grow stronger. The dissonance becomes more pronounced, like an irritating buzzing in the soul. Many of us attempt not to listen to it. We work harder. We use substances, hobbies, material possessions, and relationships to dull the growing voices of our souls. We look for external earmuffs to drown out the soul's messages. But the dissonance will not be muffled. It comes from within. The only way to stop the cacophony is to go within ourselves, to stop and be quiet and truly learn to know ourselves as we really are—not as the persons others have always told us we were. Our society, however, praises external achievement, not internal reflection, so many people do not listen to the dissonance. This refusal to listen and attempts to drown out the soul's voice is sometimes called *mid-life crisis.*

Mike arrived at the therapy office one evening coming straight from the hospital. A well-known plastic surgeon, he was recognized in the community for the fine work he did restructuring the broken faces and bodies of accident and burn victims. Mike had been married since medical school. His wife was a family practice physician. She worked half-time and spent the other half of her working life as the mother of their six-year-old twins.

Mike drove a low green imported sports car. His appearance would have graced a Hollywood screen. Perfect features, wavy black hair, beautiful silk suit and tie, and soft leather shoes.

Mike sank into the couch in the office, put his hands over his face and shuddered. The therapist sat quietly, trying to imagine why a man so successful in life was asking for emotional support. Finally he spoke. "I should be a happy man. I have a wonderful wife, two beautiful children and a highly successful career. Still I wake in the night thinking of suicide. Why am I so miserable"?

Mike told more of his story. He was the only child of a surgeon. From birth, he had been destined to go to medical school. His father had enjoyed reasonable success, but Mike always knew that his task in life was to become famous. At thirty-six years of age, he had already accomplished more than local fame.

He had married another physician, much to his parents' delight, and they had duly produced adorable children.

But Mike felt a great gulf of loneliness in his life. He could not identify its source, but he was sure of its depth and width—"too deep and wide to cross to find myself." The therapist was fascinated by this description of feeling separated from himself. He said that some days he felt like a walking, talking robot. Sometimes, he did not even enjoy his work. This was interesting because he was convinced that he really did want to be a plastic surgeon. In fact, Mike was especially troubled because he knew that there wasn't any part of his life he was willing to give up. That must mean he loved all those aspects of his life! Why could he not feel happy?

Through therapy, Mike was able to confirm that the external components of his life were all aspects he wanted to keep. What was missing was a sense of himself in all those things. He felt, rather, that they had been all parts of his parents' plan. Because of this feeling, Mike had never really invested himself emotionally in his marriage or in a relationship with his children. He had, instead, spent most of his time and energy building his career, coming home only when he was exhausted. His wife filled in nicely as a parent and the children had learned "not to bother Daddy because he is tired from working so much." His life had become completely unbalanced.

As Mike allowed himself to develop relationships with his family, he began to find that he truly enjoyed time with them. At first, it was difficult to reorganize his medical practice and teach his colleagues that he would not be available twenty-four hours, seven days a week. He began to receive feedback from his wife and children about how much they enjoyed time with him. Mike became more motivated to give them more of himself. Finally, he developed a balance between relationships at home and at work. He was able to remain in the profession he loved and at which he was exceptionally talented. And he had a happy family life.

Because so much of our self-identity is tied up in our professional lives as caregivers, when we find that our lives are not working, the realization is agonizing. *"If I can't make it as a counselor, then who am I?" "I'm a cop; I can't imagine myself doing anything else."* Because we have derived so much of our sense of who we are by living up to other people's expectations, the thought of "letting down" those other people is frightening. *"If I choose to listen to the dissonance, to discover my soul's voice, I may discover that I do not want to be a teacher. That would mean that I am not the person everyone thinks I am. Then what will be left of me?"*

CARING FOR MYSELF AND ABOUT OTHERS– MAINTAINING BOUNDARIES

It is vital that we learn the difference between *caring for* and *caring about*. Except in exceptional circumstances, we care only for babies and the very ill who cannot care for themselves. Even then, we need a strong sense of the boundary between them and us. In normal circumstances, however, *we care about others and for ourselves*. This allows others to care for themselves as much as possible. It maintains the sense of the other's dignity and personhood. It allows the other to listen to her own soul.

As professional caregivers our task in maintaining boundaries is especially difficult because the people whose lives we touch professionally do need us to care for them in some ways. This is often complicated by the fact that many of these people want to rely completely on us and not think for or care for themselves. We need to be constantly aware of the question, "What are the appropriate boundaries between myself and this person?" The professional codes of ethics of our professional governing bodies always recommend ways we can maintain physical boundaries. However, only a healthy psyche with a strong sense of oneself can discern emotional boundaries. It is in this area of emotional boundaries that many professional caregivers lose track of the separation between themselves and others.

Certainly, caregivers are not the only group of people who often define themselves by other people's expectations and approval. Entertainers and athletes thrive on external attention. Many, many others are needful of "strokes" from those around them. But because our professions carry us into such intimate contact with the lives of others, we often lose track of the point where the others end and we begin. We forget how to care *about* others and we begin to care *for* them. We become emotionally enmeshed into our roles as caregivers and our self-images are appended to those for whom we care. Remember the "Get-Away Factor"? If you find you are having trouble separating yourself from other people's pain, or are confusing *caring about others* with *caring for others*, it's a pretty good signal your dream has gotten away from you.

When our identities are so deeply interwoven with our sense of our own ability to care for others, and because of changes in the systems within which we work, our caregiving becomes less effective or impossible—or the internal dissonance becomes so strong we can no longer ignore it—we are devastated.

Many of us learned at an early age that even if we listened to our own inner soul voice, when we tried to speak or live the message we knew to be our own, we would be unheard by those in power. This powerless position is often recognized early in life, with our parents and teachers, and then with the systems within which we live and work.

Charlene was the last of ten children in her family. As a child, she never felt close to her mother and always felt like a burden.

At times I would hear my mother tell me to get out of the way, and I took that to heart and tried to make myself invisible . . .

This is the statement of one woman, but how many of us can identify with its content? Charlene's mother's rejection drew her closer to her father and she looked for protection and acceptance from him. However, she learned an important lesson when she showed her father her eighth grade report card. She thought he would praise her, but instead his response was one of criticism.

"What happened to the other mark in spelling?" That devastated me, and from then on, I felt no matter what I did was not quite good enough. I carried the fear of authority and the need for 100% approval from authority figures into religious life [2].

Charlene became a nun and a teacher. When she found that neither her community nor the educational system heard her voice and honored her needs, she experienced inner dissonance. She tells of feeling "powerless and out of control . . . and filled with feelings of insecurity, frustration, and vulnerability" [2, p. 66].

The dissonance increased until she lost interest in continuing with life. After some major times of crisis, she entered a residential treatment center.

As Charlene progressed through therapy and began to have a sense of her true self, she said,

I have come to realize that I have not given myself the right to "be." It's that deep. I have not given myself the right to be alive. So if I don't have that right, how can I have a right to be heard. How can I have a right to be heard if I don't even have the right to live [2, p. 68].

DO I KNOW HOW TO SPEAK MY OWN SOUL'S MESSAGES?

One of the frustrations many caregivers experience in large, anonymous systems is a sense of our own inability to speak up and tell what we need. Sometimes this is because the system simply will not respond. More often, it is because we do not know how to speak clearly and loudly to authority figures. Our poor sense of who we are, coupled with the fact that most of our self-identity is tied up in our ability to work as caregivers, makes us especially vulnerable to the system, and needy of approval from those who represent it.

The combination of *feeling voiceless* and *an inordinate need for approval from a disapproving system* compounds the inner dissonance and finally, our souls cry out. Something needs to happen to urge us to listen. Usually, becoming ill gets our attention. When we become sick, we are forced to slow down and listen to the soul's voice. At this point, many of us use activities or substances to help us not listen to the soul's voice.

If we do not muffle the soul's voice in alcohol, good works, or other addictive behaviors—we will begin to find ourselves.

THE EVOLUTION OF CAREGIVING DREAMS

One of the problems with an individual defining himself almost completely by his professional identity—"I am a teacher."—"I am a nurse."—is that there is no ability for that person to grow out of his original dream. Not many generations ago, a fifty-year-old person was considered aged. Now, many people return to graduate school and change professional directions even after they have reached the half-century mark in age.

Some dreams are perfectly good for a certain stage of the individual's life development. Like a snake growing out of its skin, many people grow out of their original dreams. The snake grows a new skin inside the old one, so it will not have to crawl away from the old one naked. For many people, around middle age, a new dream begins to form even before the old dream has been shed. This phenomenon may be very frightening and may cause the dreamer to hide from the new dream.

Edward was a highly successful teacher of English literature in a prestigious private school. After seventeen years in the classroom, his senior students elected him "teacher of the year." As he stood to receive his award at the graduation, everyone thought he was crying because of his joy. Actually, he was weeping because he knew that he would be leaving teaching. He had shared that reality only with his wife.

Over the past five years, Edward had found that his interests had moved away from the environment of the school. After volunteering at a shelter for street teens, he found he could not get his mind off the plight of those kids, and the pain they had experienced in their young lives. He wanted to learn how to help them more effectively and had applied to graduate school to study counseling psychology. But he felt ashamed to tell his students and colleagues. He felt like a deserter. He was also afraid that he would not be as successful at his new career. Yet he could no longer stay in the upper middle-class classroom which a few years ago he had found so stimulating and exciting.

The morning after the graduation banquet, Edward dropped into the office of the school counselor. Gradually, he shared what had been happening to his dream. He shared his fears and insecurity. "It's as if I must move on, but when I leave here, I'll be leaving behind a large part of who I am." The counselor helped him think of the possibility that he had, for several years, been discovering new aspects of himself—of who he was— in the ways he related at the shelter.

"This," said the counselor, "is a natural progression in human development across the life span." As Edward began to reframe his dream within this positive thought, he began to look forward to discovering more about himself in this new stage of his life.

THE EVOLUTION OF INSTITUTIONAL OR CORPORATE DREAMS

Just as personal dreams may evolve developmentally, the corporate dreams of institutions may change. An example of this corporate evolution on a very large scale is the evolving sense of many citizens of Canada that there needs to be political separation between Quebec and the rest of the country. If this becomes the belief of a majority of Quebecois, that province will secede from the country, taking with it all its citizens, whether they want this change or not. For many Canadians in all provinces, this evolution feels very uncomfortable.

The vision of a care-giving institution may also evolve over time, especially with changes in leadership and economic realities. This evolution can leave many people feeling uncomfortable working in the changed institutional environment. If the changes have come about without the caregiver's voice being requested or heard by those in leadership, the dissonance within the caregiver may cause a strong enough sense of discomfort that he needs to change. Sometimes, this change will mean looking for another environment in which to live one's dream. Sometimes it may call for a complete change in one's self-definition as a professional.

The Canadian government and Concordia College[1] recognized the reality that for many people in medical professions, economic cutbacks have meant that there simply are not enough jobs available for nurses. They have addressed that reality with their program *Redesigning Dreams: A Transition Series for Nursing Professionals.*[2] In the section of the program which supports nurses in finding new jobs, Rozak compares the search to the common nursing experience of starting an IV.

> Some jobs are easy to get but you may or may not be interested in them, some appear as if they're going to be easier to get than they are, others are more of a challenge to find in the hidden job market, and still others seem to be a sure bet but end up being dead end roles or disappear completely [3, p. 5].

Rozak says that Step 1 to *Hitting Your Employment Vein* lies in revisiting your heart and asking yourself the questions:

[1] The Center For Career Development Innovation (C.C.D.I.) at Concordia College & Human Resources Development Canada.

[2] Project conceived of by Maryanne Kuzio, Canada Employment Center Program Officer and written by Lorna Rozak and Anne Smith. For information, please contact Canada Employment Center, Edmonton South, Edmonton, Alberta, Canada.

• Have I begun to address my job loss and worked through most of my anger and sadness?
• Do I have a sense of my mission?
• Do I have a sense of my ideal job?
• Do I have a clear sense of who I am?

We believe that these self-questions are valuable not only for the professional whose position has disappeared because of institutional evolution, but also for those of us who find that our satisfaction with our work has drastically lessened. Our only change in these questions would be in the order in which they need to be asked. Until I have a reasonably clear sense of who I am (the last question above), it seems that I will have a difficult task to answer the other three questions in my own voice.

Rozak states her last question in respect to acing interviews by knowing ". . . what you want and what you have to offer. How can you market yourself effectively if you don't know what you've got that is of value?" [3, pp. 10-11]. We would add that we cannot decide where to market ourselves until we know who we are and have listened to our hearts. The question, "Who am I?" needs to precede all others. Only when one has deep awareness of one's own unique personhood and dreams can one decide where to plant those dreams and nurture them to fruition.

VALUES DISSONANCE

One of the most painful situations exists when the ethical values of the individual cannot be lived out in the reality of the institution. Disillusionment with systems leads us to question our dreams which are embedded within the system.

Jim was one of five associate pastors of a very large church in an affluent neighborhood. He had chosen to become professionally associated with this congregation because he believed that the Biblical and Gospel values were the basis of their belief system. For Jim, part of Gospel values meant an awareness of, and outreach to, the less fortunate members of society.

For his first three years at the church, Jim was busily enthralled with becoming a useful part of the ministry team. He worked actively with the youth group and conducted adult education classes. The friendliness and caring of this church enfolded him and he became aware of his growing feeling that he had "come home" professionally and personally.

After three years, Jim believed that he had proven his competence and wanted a greater share in the planning of programs, especially where they touched his ministries. He decided to have the youth group experience a broader segment of society that their white middle-class neighborhood offered. He planned a field trip to an AIDS hospice and another to a daycare facility for inner-city children.

A few days before the first field trip, Jim was called into the office of the senior pastor, who explained that he had been receiving calls from parents who did not want their children exposed to the "seamy elements" of society. Jim expected the pastor to say, "I just want you to be aware of this, but I'm behind you and will support you with the direction you are going." Instead, he asked Jim to cancel all field trips, unless they were to neighboring churches whose theology was similar to their own. He was to concentrate his ministry on "teaching the Biblical values of family life and clean living."

Jim felt hurt but decided to take his pastor's advice. However, from that day on, he saw church activities with a different eye. He noticed that the senior pastor lived an affluent life and even the five associates were paid high salaries with excellent benefits, such as luxurious paid vacations and church-owned vehicles for their personal use.

Jim began to visit other churches in his time off work. He saw that most pastoral professionals were living much less affluent lifestyles and that other churches sponsored soup kitchens, refugees, and ministry to the sick. He began to think that the ministry thrust of his church was inward, not out into society, except in areas where new people were possibly attracted to the church. Jim realized that he was becoming thoroughly disillusioned with his church and his own ministry.

"I should be able to inspire these kids and their parents to see beyond their own noses," he chided himself. But he noticed that the Sunday sermons often were aimed at target groups who did not meet the theological specifications of the senior pastor, so were judged unacceptable.

Jim began to lose energy for his work. His wife, Susan, became concerned because the spring was gone from his step and he displayed no excitement about his church activities. He became more and more critical about the church and that criticism and negativity flowed over onto Susan and their children. Jim developed headaches and a stiff back.

Finally, Susan persuaded Jim to speak with a counselor from the Employee Assistance Department at her place of employment. The counselor listened as Jim shared his disillusionment, and then asked, "So what are you willing to do to feel better about your professional life and yourself as a professional?" This question started Jim's healing process. He gradually became ready to resign from the church and found another job until he felt ready to explore other options for ministry. He let Susan in on his struggles and she supported him. He re-evaluated his vision for his own ministry and decided to renew his faith in it and in himself as a pastoral professional. All of this took nearly a year.

Today, Jim is the pastor of a smaller church in a working-class neighborhood. His church is becoming known as one which welcomes and responds to the needs of anyone who comes to its door. He has to buy his own car and he and his family live in a comfortable apartment near the church. He will tell you that leaving the large affluent high profile church was the best career move he ever made, and also the most painful.

The problem in this situation was not that either Jim, or the church with which he was affiliated, had inappropriate or wrong values. The problem, for Jim, was that his values were different from those of the church, and that these differences were creating a dissonance in his soul.

QUESTIONS FOR REFLECTION: UNDERSTANDING MY DREAM TO GIVE CARE

1. List three things you feel to be true about yourself. Do you appreciate or dislike these three things?
2. Make a list of your talents. Now go down the list again and write beside each:
   - the reasons you believe you have these talents;
   - the people who have pointed out these talents to you;

- places and times you use these talents;
- on a scale of 1-10, where 10 is high, the amount of enjoyment you have from these talents.

3. What people or life circumstances have helped you in, or prevented you from, recognizing and listening to the voice of your soul?
4. Are there other voices inhabiting your soul place? Whose voices are they?
5. If there are other people's voices in your soul place, are you willing to give these voices back to the persons to whom they belong, making a place for your soul's authentic voice?
6. On a scale of 1-10, where 10 is "absolute," what is your commitment to cleaning inauthentic voices out of your soul's home?
7. If you know your own soul's voice, are you able to speak it and be heard in your professional institutional realities? Why or why not? What might help?

REFERENCES

1. R. F. J. Jevne and H. W. Zingle, *Striving for Health: Living with Broken Dreams,* Alberta School Employee Benefit Plan and University of Alberta, Edmonton, 1992.
2. B. Laframboise, *Finding Voice: The Psychosocial Process of Healing Wounded Women,* Religious, doctoral dissertation, Department of Educational Psychology, Faculty of Education, University of Alberta, 1993.
3. L. J. Rozak, Reaching Your Target; A Job Search Guide, Part 3 of *Redesigning Dreams: A Transition Series for Nursing Professionals,* Human Resources Development Canada, Edmonton, 1994.

CHAPTER 6

When Dreams Don't Work

HEART LABOR

When I work too hard and then lie down,
even my sleep is sad and all worn out.
You want me to name the specific sorrows?
They do not matter. You have your own.
Most of the people in the world
go out to work, day after day,
with their voices chained in their throats.
I am swimming a narrow, swift river.
Upstream, the clouds have already darkened
and deep blue holes I cannot see
churn up under the smooth flat rocks.
The Greeks have a word, *paropono*,
for the complaint without answer,
for how the heart labors, while
all the time our faces appear calm
enough to float through in the moonlight.

Maggie Anderson [1, p. 14]

Reprinted by permission of the University of Pittsburgh Press

If you are reading this book, you already realize that sometimes even the best-intentioned dreams don't work. Sometimes,
as we have seen, this happens because the dreamer has been
trying to live someone else's dream.

I was brought up to be a very docile little girl who does what
she's told and what she's expected to do [2, p. 14].

She's a _____ teacher. And my father's a ____. And so
they feel that I'm doing all right. I just flatly outright told

her I had to come to terms with her last year and say you
know, you've got to let me lead my life. You can't lead it for
me [2, p. 119].

Other times, the dream may be one which realistically could
work, but someone other than the dreamer would be the right
one to carry it out. Many dreams are not meant to be harvested
by the same people who plant them. Sometimes this is because a
dream takes a long time between gestation and fruition. Other
times, it needs more than one person's talents and insights to
nurture its growth. Ronna played a major role in developing the
Department of Counseling and Psychology at a cancer hospital,
and then moved on, leaving to others the leadership role in that
dream. She realized that her passions were shifting as were her
life circumstances. She wanted to honor new limits, new interests, and new adventures. Also, the dream needed to live on its
own, to have its own identity, fueled by the drive of new blood.
For both Ronna and the dream she had contributed to birthing,
it was time to move on.

Sometimes, the dream is just not appropriate to or supported
by the system in which it is planted. A police officer told of his
disillusionment with detective work, "You bring in the per-
petrator and they admit their guilt because they know they
won't do time. These days, if they do any time at all, you think
you're successful. Unless they've threatened public safety by a
violent act, they'll get public service hours or some other token
punishment. And they'll be back on the streets stealing cars or
committing other non-violent crimes within days."

Qualities of the dream—rigidity, narrowness or breadth,
realism or fantasy—may all contribute in part to its success or
failure.

It is never one aspect of the dream which pulls the dreamer
down into burnout, but a combination of several factors (see
Figure 1). An individual may plant a dream in a system which is
open to new thoughts and ideas, but which is underfunded with
personnel to carry out the new vision. The dream may be
authentic to the dreamer and flexible, but the dreamer may lack
the patience and ongoing hope to allow the system to gear up
gradually to implement the dream. Together, the problematic

PERSONAL DREAM FACTORS	SYSTEMIC FACTORS
• authenticity • timing • energy • rigidity/flexibility • self-discipline • self-esteem • patience • commitment/hope	• control issues • flexibility/rigidity • openness to new thoughts and ideas • commitment to employee health • funding

Figure 1. Dream aspects contributing to caregiver health or burnout.

factors work to begin a process of disillusionment, emotional and cognitive dissonance, and depersonalization.

THE PROCESS OF BURNOUT

Denying the Signs

The progress of developing burnout is often unsuspected and insidious. This may be because caregivers cling tenaciously to their ideals and do not interpret their growing disillusionment as signs of burnout. Also, because the causes of developing burnout are rarely cut and dried, its process may be easily denied until one day, suddenly, the individual can no longer cope. Often, there are signs of approaching debilitation, which are either unrecognized or are denied by the dreamer and/or those around her.

> I think people don't realize it's happening until it's too late. I didn't think I was as bad as I was [2, p. 22].

> Everybody thought I was doing a great job yet inside I dreaded every day. I was rewarded for my magnificent performance by . . . Things inside me got worse. I finally got so stressed . . . I passed out . . . I thought this was the end [2, p. 23].

We caregivers believe we are the strong ones. Other people come to us for help. We don't think of ourselves as also vulnerable. Because so much of our sense of self-identity is tied up in our professional roles, to acknowledge an inner sense of dissonance, a lessening of attachment to the professional role, would mean acknowledging to others that we also have needs. For many people, that admission connotes, "I don't have it all together. I am inadequate." People don't want to hear me say that and I don't even want to think it.

Steve had been a cop for thirteen years. In his time on the force, he had seen a lot of changes. It seemed that every year, things on the streets got tougher and more violent. The thought that he might actually need to shoot and kill someone seemed less wearing on him than the everyday calls to domestic violence situations and the constant effort to maintain his sense of pride in his profession in the light of public criticism of law enforcement professionals.

The year he turned forty, Steve began to feel edgy. Work demanded that he put on a tough face. Realistically, he didn't see a lot of nice people when he was working. In fact, he saw a whole lot of people who were not very nice. He could cope with that. He and his colleagues knew how to deal with people who were not nice, even though financial constraints were making it harder and harder to do the job. What Steve found most difficult was the necessary change in personality between work and home. At work, he needed to be untrusting, cynical, and tough. At home, he needed to be a supportive, loving husband and father to three teenagers. Steve was having an increasingly difficult time keeping those different roles straight. More and more often, he "pulled rank" on family members, greeting them with hard-nosed cynicism instead of caring attention. He thought about old western movies, where the gunfighters would hang up their holsters at the door of the saloon and then get into fistfights at the bar.

Steve's wife and children tried to ask him for more appropriate attention, but he could not admit to them what he saw as weakness and incompetence. So they began to emotionally withdraw from him. His wife, a nurse, volunteered to work more hours, spending less time at home. The kids found lots to keep them busy and away. Steve felt less pressure when they didn't bother him for attention. He could reinvest in work. He could really clamp down on some people who needed to be clamped down on.

Two crises happened the same day. At ten o'clock on a Tuesday morning, the school called to tell him his sixteen-year-old son had come that day with a hunting knife and Steve's immediate presence was requested. Humiliated and angry, Steve drove his expelled son home and left him at the house, saying they would finish their business that evening. He drove back to the police station and was called into his captain's office because a suspect he had arrested in a drug bust had complained that Steve punched him in front of witnesses as he was being arrested. Steve was told that he would be riding a desk instead of a police car until an investigation had been completed.

Steve left the station and went to a bar. He stayed there several hours, until the bartender called a taxi and sent him home. He did not remember that ride or arriving home and going to bed. The next morning, he knew that he could not go back to work. He did not want to see his family. He just wanted to stay in bed.

Steve's process of disillusionment and detachment happened gradually, over several years. It did not happen for one reason. Many factors contributed to form a life situation where he was not able to find touchstones for what he thought police work should be like or even for who he wanted to be as a police officer. His self-identity was so firmly entrenched in the image of the uniform and badge, that it was extremely difficult to acknowledge his growing disillusionment. In fact, while their professions are very different, Steve's experience was not so different from that of Susan, a surgeon and single parent of two boys. Susan told her story this way.

"My parents were immigrants fleeing Europe after World War II. I was born in America and nearly every day as I was growing up, my parents would tell me how fortunate I was to be living in a country where if I worked hard and was honest, I could have anything I wanted.

"My second semester at university, I decided to major in pre-med classes. I did work hard and I was honest. It seemed that my parents were right. I graduated from medical school near the

top of my class and was offered a position at a prestigious university hospital. I can still remember how proud my parents were at my graduation. Every relative from all over the country was there. I was the first doctor in the family.

"As soon as I completed my residency, I was offered a staff position here at _____. I've never wanted to leave. I never saw myself as anything other than a front line surgeon.

"What I didn't count on was the constant bombardment of horrible and hopeless cases. I became a doctor to save lives. I invested over ten years of my life training to do it well. But over and over again, I have to tell patients or their families that I can't save them. And so many of those cases are the result of unnecessary situations—drug habits, accidents caused by alcohol, and domestic abuse. Last week, a convicted murderer was sent to us and we had to treat him the same way we would treat your mother or child. But that doesn't bother me as much as having to face the families, day after day, and tell them their loved one can't be helped. I just force myself to stop feeling and get on with the job. Then, when I have a day off, my family wants quality time. I don't blame them; I'm home so seldom. But it's really hard to lose the hospital feeling and become Mom in an hour. I take long showers and pray that the warm water will warm me up emotionally.

"It's not all glamour like those TV doctor shows. Mostly it hurts a lot and many days I wish I'd become a teacher or a business woman—anything but a doctor. Of course, it would make no sense to throw away all my training and experience at this stage. So I keep on keeping on. That's how it feels."

Susan's disillusionment with her career has permeated her life. Right now, she is just "keeping on keeping on," moving through each day like an emotionless robot, not feeling the painful realities of life in an acute care hospital.

Unfortunately, when we turn off one kind of emotion, usually, our psyches turn off other emotions as well. We lose our creative energy and stop feeling hope and joy as well as pain. Many of us need help to turn off the pain, so we use more work, alcohol and other drugs, relationships, sex, or any of a host of compulsive behaviors to sedate ourselves. Often, these become tools for our denial of the burnout process. Even when others see what is happening, many of us deny it. "People saw it and told me and I didn't believe them. I said, forget it. I can cope" [2, p. 24].

Coming to Acknowledge Symptoms

Some people, like Steve, need to crash and burn before they will admit their level of pain. For others, a day arrives when their capacity for denial is overcome by the obvious. The painful emotions which have been held down begin to rise to the surface of awareness, often with a vengeance. Symptoms of depression may set in. Eating and sleeping become either difficult to do or difficult to resist. Worry takes over the day and sleep may be disturbed by nightmares. Bouts of crying and panic attacks are common. Despair may set in. "I started thinking of having suicidal tendencies . . . I would get so tired my whole body felt like it was collapsing inside of me" [2, p. 29].

Physical symptoms, from digestive problems to headaches, often loom large at this stage of the process. Concentration is difficult and people become more susceptible to all sorts of accidents.

It is no wonder that people often become depressed at the point in burnout where it is impossible to avoid looking at the realities of life—the disillusionment with earlier dreams which had seemed so bright and shiny. As caregivers, so much of our sense of who we are has been tied up in the dreams, that we feel like all the parameters of our lives are slipping away. A critical care nurse said it this way:

> The doctors would do rounds and they'd be asking me questions and I'd be giving rote answers and inside my head, another cynical voice would be saying, "Oh sure, ask a nurse for the answers and then go back to your office and send a big bill to the patient for your services." I'd go home and stand in the shower for an hour, until the water was cold and then I'd towel off, and for a few minutes that coldness would bring me back to some contact with life. One day when a patient was transferred and I had a vial half full of valium, I just stood there holding that little bottle and thinking how it

could help me get through the night and nobody'd be any wiser. That's when I knew I needed help.

Feeling Less

When our life dreams are crumbling, when we are no longer sure who we are, many of us report the experience of feeling *less*—less enthusiastic and idealistic, less valued, less able, and less connected. This experience of diminishment sifts through all areas of life.

> I am, of course, accountable to everyone in the system, including the students. But doubt often exists in my own mind, about who is accountable to me [2, p. 29].

> So there I was, running into a burning building with two other people, and none of us thought (the person giving the orders) gave a damn about us or our safety. He had made it clear that our job was to make him look good.
>
> *a fire fighter's experience*

> I know that in the last two years, at least, that I worked, that I was not doing as good a job as I was capable of doing, mostly due to fatigue & chronic pain. This was most frustrating. I'm a good teacher, and felt that I was really inadequate [2, p. 34].

> I started to withdraw. I didn't want to talk to anybody . . . I felt a real withdrawal [2, p. 35].

> When I'd go home at the end of the day, I'd have so much from the day I was carrying around, I'd just want my husband to leave me alone. Then when I'd go to work again, I kept hoping that alarm wouldn't go off. I read stupid romances and played a few card games and went over the gear for the shift about ten times. I'd just ignore them when they spoke to me. I used to have a sense of humor, but I started to glare at them if they teased me.
>
> *medical rescue professional*

Rarely do we slow down at this time to assess what is happening. Most of us attempt to hang in there, hoping that things will change, that we're just going through a bad stage and tomorrow things will look better. We drag ourselves to work and we attempt to connect with our friends and families. Sometimes, we attempt to make a change, to a different position within the system, a different grade to teach. We may join a gym or take a Hawaiian vacation or a six-month leave of absence. These are only band-aid therapies, aimed at the symptoms of something much deeper. They don't work. Things don't change and we become more disillusioned and isolated.

Being Declared Surplus

While most people feel less valued at this time, those who experience the deepest, most profound sense of being devalued, are those whose jobs disappear. We have invented terms for the experience—"early retirement," "golden handshake," "reorganization"—euphemisms for the reality that you aren't wanted or needed any more.

> I have never been unemployed and found this experience almost humiliating . . . declared surplus. Returned as a permanent substitute. Made to feel as though there was a "Hit List" [2, p. 32].

Often this happens very suddenly. A person who has built his whole life around a job is told that he does not have that job anymore. He may not have been aware of any previous disillusionment or isolation. Suddenly, his reality has completely changed. Greg, a nurse, tells of his experience.

> We knew there were going to be cutbacks . . . But I thought I'd be safe because they needed male nurses and I had a lot of specialized experience. What I didn't realize was that they were closing my whole department, consolidating with (another hospital), and for orthopedic nurses, their people had first choice of the jobs. When she told me, I just stood there with my mouth open. I'd been so sure I'd be safe!

Recognizing the Grief

Finally, a deep sadness must be acknowledged. There is no way to run from or deny the reality that our dreams have died. We are no longer young idealists ready to change and save the world. The pain and injustice of life have caught up with us, and our dreams lie in tatters about us. Our professional life, our personal relationships, and even our sense of self, have fallen apart. We are exhausted and we feel the absence of creative energy to begin again. Not uncommonly, anger and fear are followed by deep sadness.

Mourning the death of a dream is really no different from mourning the death of a beloved person. It may, in fact, impact the griever more deeply because our dreams are part of how we perceive ourselves. This is not about the death of another person, but about the painful amputation of a part of oneself. The dream, so much a part of who you are, is gangrenous. If you cannot allow its amputation, you are at risk for your very life. You must lay to rest the old dream, remove your emotional investments in its role in your life, and prepare to create a new dream which will work for your present life reality.

The immensity of this realization can cause multiple emotional, spiritual, and physical symptoms. Lack of energy and creativity, disinterest in food, recreation, and sex, headaches and digestive disorders, back pain and muscular aches, and withdrawal from ordinary life activities are all normal.

Table 1 lists many of the symptoms of burnout grief. Most people will not experience all of the symptoms, but everyone will experience several.

Grief is a process for bridging the gap between something which is gone and something which will be. Figure 2 calls these things the *Old Reality* and the *New Reality*.

Now that we understand that the syndrome we have been calling burnout is actually a profound sense of mourning for the death of our dreams, we can understand that healing from burnout will come from entering into the grief process and allowing that process to build bridges toward the new realities which will become parts of our new dreams.

Table 1. Symptoms of Burnout Grief

Emotional	Physical	Spiritual
• Deep sense of sadness • Loss of interest in work, personal life • Loss of sexual interest • Nightmares • Sense of hopelessness • Angry outbursts • Motivational difficulty • Lack of creativity • Fear • Paranoia • Crying bouts • Anxiety and fear • Agitation and sluggishness • Death (suicide) ideation	• Sleep disturbances • Headaches • Back and muscular pain • Digestive upsets • Lessened immunity to common infections • Sexual dysfunction	• Anger at other people and at God • Withdrawal from faith and community activities • Difficulty praying • Hopelessness • Fear • Diminished creativity • Sense of loneliness, isolation

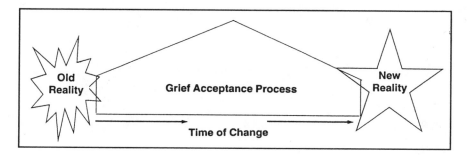

Figure 2. The grief process.

RECOGNIZING MY BURNOUT SYMPTOMS

1. On a 10-point scale, where 10 is very much and 1 is hardly at all, how much did I look forward to arriving at work this morning?
2. When someone asks, "How are you?," if I answered them honestly, what would I say today?
3. If, three years from now, you feel the way you do today, how OK will that be? (You may want to place this on a 10-point scale.)
4. Am I experiencing any early warning burnout signals— colds . . . headaches . . . chest pain . . . crankiness . . . fatigue?
5. What symptom or condition would cause me to say, "This is enough. Something has to change!"

REFERENCES

1. M. Anderson, Heart Labor, in *A Space Filled With Moving,* University of Pittsburgh Press, Pittsburgh, Pennsylvania, 1992.
2. R. F. J. Jevne and H. W. Zingle, *Striving for Health: Living with Broken Dreams,* Alberta School Employee Benefit Plan and University of Alberta, Edmonton, 1992.

CHAPTER 7

A Time to Heal from Broken Dreams

...for real happiness arises from the unassailable sense that you are free to create your own life. . . . *The feeling of inward freedom is everyone's birthright* [1, p. 12].

I'm so glad to know that there is hope—that the way I am feeling now can be time-limited. Some days, it feels as if I'm in a box canyon, with no way out except through the entrance that brought me to this point in the first place. Now you're telling me that this is actually a very deep valley, and that not only is there a way out, but there may even be several options. You have given me something to cling to. You have given me hope.

a physician recovering from burnout

Options. Hope. When it seems as if your life is falling apart, when your emotions and your body are exhausted, when the illusions around which your life has been built are turning to disillusion—how is it possible to find the energy and creativity to continue the journey?

I'm forty-three years old. Since I was eight, I wanted to be a fire fighter. I AM a fire fighter. It's all I know how to do, all I want to do. Now you're telling me my nerves are shot. What does that mean to you? You say, "Your nerves are shot, man." You might as well say, "Your life is shot." Because I have nothing left to live for. My nerves are shot because of all the s—t I've had to take from the system, and now the system is throwing me away.

a fire fighter taking early retirement

101

For many caregivers, the professional and personal aspects of identity are deeply integrated. It is hard to understand who one is without the familiar professional aspects of self-image.

> Professionalism has so many dimensions to me. But I'm interpreting it to do with the meaning of work life for me. It's so pervasive. It covers my entire life and being. . . . There's no clean line between the personal and the professional [2, p. 49].

Unraveling the two aspects of self-image and discovering one's personhood aside from the professional may be a laborious and exhausting task. When the person is already emotionally depleted or ill, finding the energy and creativity to do this may seem almost impossible. Grieving for the lost ability to function as one had before can invoke fear. Robb tells of the sense of empowerment which goes with many professions.

> . . . a part of our professionalism is the continuing empowerment of ourselves . . . as we become increasingly able to do our work, congruent in our work and confident in our abilities. When we become empowered, we become more self-accepting of our deeper selves. We gain courage to act in ways that are more spontaneous and more reflective of who we are . . . [2, p. 49].

Losing the ability to function as a professional or to function professionally in familiar ways seems to counteract the personal empowerment which we had worked all our lives to establish. It is in direct opposition to the plans and dreams which had seemed to be our maps for life.

The journey back to health from the deeply painful experience of burnout is one of learning to accept new realities, grieving for old dreams, and reinvesting in new life possibilities. For many, it is a difficult and frightening process.

> I would say that the vast majority of my time was spent in therapeutic activities.

> One of the biggest steps I made was to become less frightened. It's like . . . two years when you train hard [3, p. 52].

The Effects of Physical Disabilities

For everyone, the first task of recovery is to admit that, in fact, there is a major health problem. Until this happens, it is impossible to ask for and receive help.

When burnout is manifested in physical as well as emotional symptoms the affected person has a double task of healing. If you are affected physically, it may be difficult to accept what your body is telling you. Physical pain, especially pain which is long-lasting or chronic, has a way of undercutting emotional coping skills. Pain can overpower even the best intentions. Many people find that pain takes over every aspect of life.

> When a person is healthy, they can cope with family problems or other stresses; when you're in constant pain, little things seem to become major problems [3, p. 60].

Occasionally, the physical disability is permanent. Emotional healing, in this case, involves reconciling oneself with, and finding hope in, the new reality.

Kim was a fire fighter, one of the first women in her department. Highly motivated, physically strong, and intelligent, she was progressing through the ranks of her profession. She was especially proud when her hometown newspaper wrote an article about her contribution to the community.

About ten years into her career, Kim began to suspect something she did not want to accept. It seemed that in her department, there was an invisible ceiling for female fire fighters. They would be promoted and given responsibility at a certain level, and no further. Several times, she found herself and female colleagues passed over for promotions for which they were qualified.

Kim approached her immediate supervisors with her suspicions. They were sympathetic but non-supportive. "The problem is," they told her, "you can't expect a bunch of macho men to take orders from a woman. It just won't work. We have to think of the morale of the whole department. It's even a safety issue."

Kim returned to her work and tried to carry on. She wanted to understand and respect the stance of her superiors. The harder she tried to understand, the more her inner voice was crying,

"This isn't right." Kim began to experience acid indigestion and frequent headaches. Sleep became difficult and this was a special problem because she needed to be wide awake whenever an alarm was sounded. Then one day, Kim noticed blood in the toilet. Her doctor diagnosed inflammatory bowel disease, a chronic condition aggravated by stress. Kim's fire fighting career was over. Both the physician and a psychologist whom she consulted recommended that she find a less stressful career.

Since the age of ten, Kim had dreamed of being a fire fighter. She could not imagine another career with as much satisfaction. She did not want to accept that she could not do that job any more. For several months, Kim followed her doctor's medical orders and worked with the psychologist. One night, waking with a pain in her gut and hurrying to the bathroom, she realized, "They're right. I can't go back to work and I can't go on like this. I need to find a new direction for my life."

Her journey to wellness and to reinvesting in life was a long one. Eventually, Kim and her husband moved to a small town, where she opened a gift shop. She still acts as a volunteer fire fighter and enjoys the contribution she makes to this community. Her career interests have shifted to her business which is very successful.

Accepting disability means grieving for what used to be—perhaps grieving for a dream that never reached fruition. One person compared this unfulfilled dream to a stillborn child.

> The dream seemed so real, and it seemed as if it was working. All those years of school, grad school, clinical training. And just when I knew I was ready to really contribute, the people with the money decided they didn't want what I had to give. I was "overqualified, too specialized." It's as if the baby I birthed was dead before the birthing. All I have is a feeling of emptiness and anger, and I feel afraid. I don't know how I can start again.
>
> *a nurse*

This sort of grief is especially painful. Dreams which have succeeded, even temporarily, at least leave us with memories of triumph, of goals reached. From those memories, we can draw hope for other dreams. A dream, however, which has never borne fruit eats away at self-assurance and increases the frustration and anger which are endemic to the grief experience.

GRIEVING THE DREAM

Whatever the reasons a dream has not worked, the dreamer who experiences burnout will be drawn into an experience of pain which one man described as feeling like a whirlpool.

> It threatened to pull me down and down, until I lost my sense of balance and felt as though I would not survive. Then I remembered the rule I learned in my kayaking class. If you tip and are pulled into a whirlpool, don't fight. Just hold your breath and relax and the whirlpool will toss you up to the surface again. So I tried to "go with the flow" of my emotions, emotionally holding my breath by not making major decisions. I attempted to relax and see where the whirlpool would take me. It seemed like an eternity. Then one day, sure enough, I realized I had come to the surface again. I could feel my balance returning and I could see the sun and feel hopeful. Having come through that, I feel sure I can handle almost any life crisis.

We often think of grief as the experience of pain when someone we love has died. Actually, we grieve any time we experience loss or change. Grieving for a life dream is like grieving for a part of oneself. All the emotions and physical responses that might be experienced when a loved one dies are just as likely to occur with burnout. Sadness, frustration, and anger are normal. Profound fatigue and loss of both appetite and sexual interest are common. You may experience more infections because the immune system, experiencing stress, cannot respond efficiently. Because grief compromises cognitive functioning, many people find that they cannot make decisions or complete intellectual tasks as well as they could before burnout.

COPING STYLES

People respond to the experiences of loss in several different ways. Some, whom we call *The Hangers-On,* will cling to the past, not wanting to admit that things have changed. Others, *The Grief-Jumpers*, will attempt to bypass the pain by jumping over the discomfort and investing immediately and deeply in the new reality. A third group, *The "What, Me Worry?" Club*, just float with the stream, never acknowledging preferences or taking positions. Finally, there are *The Survivors,* who recognize that changes are happening, allow themselves to grieve what is past, and gradually invest in new realities. Usually, a person's style of responding to different kinds of life changes will be consistent. As you read the descriptions below, try to decide in which category you fit. You may have factors of more than one style, for example, many people will hang on to the old for some time, but eventually embrace reality and move on.

The Hangers-On

These people resist recognizing the inevitable changes in their life realities. Their motto seems to be, "Not on your life!" When they do acknowledge changes, it is usually with resistance and anger. They often blame other people and seldom recognize that they have personally contributed, in any way, to the necessity for change. If we could plot them on Figure 1, we would find them clinging to the old reality with all their might and resisting angrily the movement through the time of change. These are often the folks who grouch and grumble, always upset at something the administration has decided and saying things like, "Why do we need to change. We've always done things this way. Why can't we just keep on the way we've been going?" They may be quite unpleasant to new or young employees, seeing them as agents of the new order. Sometimes, they hasten their own termination by their stubborn refusal to embrace the new, and by their resentful attitude. When this happens, it is often very sad because usually they are very committed workers. They simply have great difficulty accepting life changes. They tend not to recognize the signs of their own impending burnout, until they collapse.

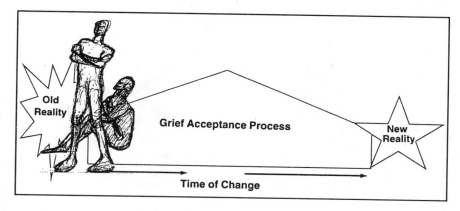

Figure 1. The Hangers-On.

The Grief-Jumpers

Another group of people will respond in just the opposite way. They will be first on the bandwagon, ushering in the changes their colleagues are resisting. Their motto is, *"I'm adaptable."* Occasionally, this is because they are truly prophetic and farsighted individuals. Usually, however, they are trying to control the situation just as much as those who are trying to resist the situation. The philosophy could be stated as, "Change is going to happen, so if I become part of the advance guard, I'll be safe and I won't need to do the grieving." These people are moving as quickly as possible toward the new reality, attempting to avoid the change process with its inherent grief (see Figure 2). If economic realities or leadership changes cause them to be laid off, they are usually stunned because they were so sure that they would be safe.

Because they habitually deny the natural human need for a time of grief and adjustment, these people often have an especially difficult time making the transition to what may be a very different life reality. Their investment in every change has actually been an attempt to hold on to whatever remained of their original dreams. When their dreams fail completely, they resist the emergence of new dreams based on new life realities. They become absolutely disillusioned and afraid to trust themselves to dream again. They may say things like, "I tried so

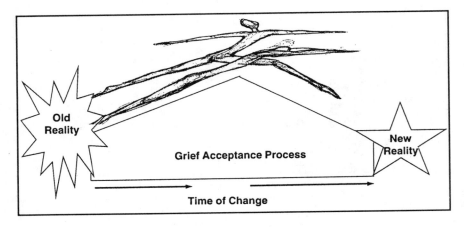

Figure 2. The Grief-Jumpers.

hard! I did everything possible and tried every avenue to make it work. Why should I try again?"

The "What, Me Worry?" Club

A third group seem to deny reality completely. They will not be part of the change process nor will they cling to the old (see Figure 3). They will emotionally separate themselves from the situation.

On the surface, these people seem a lot like the *Hangers-On,* and often they do cling to the past. In fact, they are different only in the way they express their reluctance to change. They deny that change is happening, while the *Hangers-On* protest and fight. Their disinterest may actually be an expression of a feeling of helplessness. Politically, the *Hangers-On* group will form conservative, reactionary groups, while members of The *"What, Me Worry?" Club* will spend election day on a picnic and never go near the polls.

Ironically, they may use overwork as a strategy of non-involvement, immersing themselves in so much "busy-ness" that they do not have to pay attention to what is happening around them. If they are approached by others who are concerned about difficulties or changes, they will reply with statements like, "I

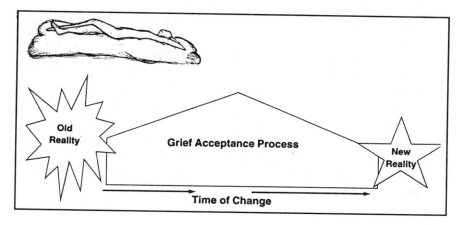

Figure 3. The "What, Me Worry?" Club.

don't have time for office politics. I'm busy. If everyone would just do their jobs and not fuss, there wouldn't be any problems." In the burnout situation, these people may have to collapse before they will accept that there is a major problem. Even if others see what is happening to them and tell them, they seldom listen, telling those who approach them to, "Mind your own business."

Working long hours, substance abuse, the acquisition of material things, gambling, and other behaviors which are destructive of themselves and others, can provide them temporary protection from reality. On our diagram, they are not even in the change picture.

The Survivors

Often the smallest group, the *Survivors* recognize that change is happening and that their own reality will be affected. They may not feel happy about the change, but they recognize that it is inevitable. They adopt the motto, "I don't wanna' but I will." Validating their own pain, they move into and through the grief process, allowing themselves to hurt and recognizing that, in time, they will adjust and find comfort in their new reality. They are able to emotionally sustain the grief process without needing to deny it or ignore it. *Survivors* can cope with the present, whatever that means. If it means they need to change and adapt, they can do so. If the present is stable and change is not happening, they enjoy the respite, recognizing that life seldom stays still for long (see Figure 4).

Because of their flexible attitude, they have good resistance to burnout, and when economic or political realities strongly affect their careers, they usually have a resilient ability to revamp or rebuild their life dreams. Often, because they are able to realistically assess and adjust to changes, they become inspired leaders.

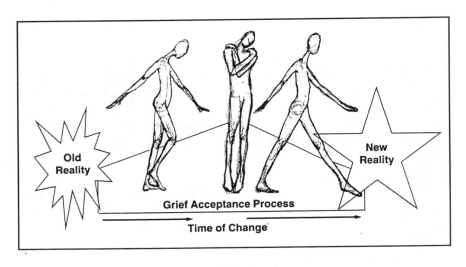

Figure 4. The Survivors.

WHO AM I?

Did you recognize yourself in any of the descriptions above? Do you *Hang-On,* happiest when things don't change and clinging to the familiar? Most of us have a little *Hanger-On* in us, often shown by the fact that we're most comfortable in old, holey jeans and a paint-spattered shirt, familiar and cozy from years of washings and wearings.

Or are you a *Grief-Jumper*, hustling along to keep up with everything new? Almost everyone, at some time, yearns to run away from the painful and find something new and better.

Are you a candidate for the *"What, Me Worry?" Club*? Do you refuse to commit to the old *or* the new, skating away and immersing yourself in whatever feels safe? Who of us hasn't played that role? Sometimes, we call this role *playing ostrich*.

How do you react when change seems inevitable? Like *The Survivors*, do you acknowledge what is happening and remain flexible for its impact on your life? Perhaps this is the ideal. For most of us, it requires some active effort. Change is usually accompanied by a natural fear of the unknown—of unanswered questions. Meeting these questions head-on can feel very risky. And in the change process is the grief, a time of intense pain. It is natural to want to avoid that pain if at all possible. *Survivors,* however, recognize that avoiding the pain is not possible and that efforts to do so are useless and often destructive.

LIFE ATTITUDES

At the core of our reactions are our *life attitudes*, which influence how we react to different aspects of life. We all have several life attitudes. Usually, they are a result of what we have learned through life experiences. Mary was mauled by a large dog when she was a child. As a middle-aged woman, she still has an attitude that large dogs are not safe and anyone who trusts them is unrealistic. Blake has always owned large, gentle dogs. He trusts them completely and has the attitude that those who do not enjoy them are just plain insensitive and silly.

Life attitudes, however, are not cemented in concrete. If Blake brought his pets to Mary's home and gradually helped her to know them, it is very possible that she could change her attitude to, "Some large dogs are gentle and can be trusted." If Blake were taken to a hospital to see a patient badly mauled by a dog, he might acknowledge, "Some large dogs are vicious and people who realize this are wise."

What life attitudes do you think would be useful ones for professional caregivers? We asked several people in a variety of caregiving roles to suggest useful and unuseful attitudes for survival. Then we plotted what they told us on Table 1. When you read this table, do you see any unuseful attitudes which you have been using for your own life?

Now, take a moment to think of other unuseful attitudes which you might be holding. It is important to consider not only what you may intellectually know to be true and healthy, but also the voices of others that speak in your soulplace and that control the actual ways you live your life. Write them into the left side of Table 2. On the right side of Table 2, write other, more useful attitudes which roughly correspond with the not-useful ones you have written. What is it about the more useful attitudes that allows for more life flexibility? Is it something about self-acceptance and care? Usually, the more we accept ourselves and allow ourselves to be human, with needs and limitations, the more ability we have to adapt to life's difficulties.

LIVING THE LOSS—
ACCEPTING THE HEALING PROCESS

Tom and Mary bought a house. They spent several months scouting the different areas of the city, carefully considering aspects of each neighborhood that would assure that their house would be more than a home—it would be an investment. They wanted to bring up their family in that home and then sell at a profit, using that profit as retirement income. They lived in the house for twenty years, each spring planning improvements which would increase the house's value and maintain their investment well.

For their anniversary, in the twenty-first year they lived in the house, they went on a dream vacation to the Caribbean. Relaxing by the blue sea, they listened to the radio news. Suddenly, both of them sat up straight. The announcer was speaking of a devastating earthquake in their home city. Seventy-five percent of all buildings were destroyed.

As soon as they could get a flight, Tom and Mary returned home. Driving from the airport, they marveled at the devastation the earthquake had wrought. Where there had previously been a beautiful city, there was now mainly rubble. Turning into their

Table 1. Life Attitudes

Unuseful Attitudes	Useful Attitude

• I need to help or "save" everyone every day.
• I am only successful if:
  – I get rich
  – All my stusdents succeed
  – All my patients (clients) get well
  – I never make a mistake
  – I am a hero
  – I publish
• When something goes wrong, it is likely because I was incompetent to control it. Therefore, I am responsible.
• I am powerless to change things I do not like.
• If my career does not work out the way I expect it to (the way I dream it), I am a failure. My professional life is over.
• Other people are more clever than I and do not mess up as much as I do. This shows that I am incompetent.
	• I want to help some people each day.
	• I can count myself successful if:
	  – I can support myself comfortably
	  – My students (patients, clients), respect me and know I respect them
	  – I learn from my mistakes
	  – I work safely and competently
	  – I enjoy my work
	• When something goes wrong, it may be because I am not in complete control of the world and some things just go wrong. I do not need to take responsibility for whatever happens.
	• I may not be able to change everything, but I can certainly exert influence in many situations.
	• If my career does not go as I am dreaming, there are other ways I can use my talents and creativity.
	• Other people also make mistakes and have failures and rejections. I am no less competent than most people.

Table 2. My Attitudes

My Less-than-Useful Attitudes	More Useful Attitudes

street, their hearts sank. The dream house they had so carefully chosen and cared for through many years was gone. Only a pile of bricks and shattered beams lay where their home had been.

How do you think Tom and Mary felt? What emotions might have controlled their lives for the next few weeks or months? Sadness? Depression? Anger? Frustration? Fear?

The loss of a dream can elicit many emotions. Just as Tom and Mary lost their dream house, the professional caregiver experiencing burnout is losing a dream in which much time, energy, money, and love have been invested. It is important that people experiencing burnout come to understand themselves as mourners. The healing process is one which acknowledges grief and supports the process of disinvestment of emotional energy from the old dream and the rebuilding of a dream which is realistic for the individual's life realities.

THE EXPERIENCE OF ANGER

Unfortunately, in contemporary Western society, we learn to deny certain emotions that have a negative connotation. Those with the strongest negative connotations are the emotions commonly experienced when we have a major loss. Likely, the most negative connotations of all are centered on the emotion which many people have been taught to deny absolutely—anger! Yet anger is a very common emotion felt by those experiencing burnout.

It is perfectly normal to feel angry when something we desire has been denied. Anger is a normal emotional response when we learn that a dream in which we have deeply invested is not going to happen.

This type of anger is especially difficult when there is no person or thing at whom it can be aimed, no target for the feelings we are experiencing. We ask ourselves the question, "At what (whom) am I angry?" We tell ourselves (or are told by others), "Don't be angry. Anger won't solve anything." But we *are* angry.

Anger does not like to be denied. It will not go away until you notice it and listen to it. If you refuse to do so, it may seem to disappear. But it is just hiding and sometime in the future it will return, perhaps disguised as depression or as physical illness.

If you are feeling angry, acknowledge that fact. Allow yourself some time to sit with the anger and feel it. Get to know it. Allow it to be, even if there is no person or thing at whom you can direct it. It may help you if you acknowledge that you don't need a specific target for the anger; you can just be angry with the situation that has brought about your sense of helplessness, your frustration, and your sadness. Your spirit is deeply wounded. That feels terrible. That is enough reason to be angry.

Imagine Tom and Mary standing in front of the rubble of their dream house. In your imagination, place your damaged dream where their house once stood. Imagine yourself standing in their place. Feel the emotions which move through your being. There are no rules about how you should feel. What is important is that you allow yourself to validate whatever emotions you are feeling.

TIME FOR HEALING

> There is a time for everything, and a season for every activity under heaven:
> a time to be born and a time to die, a time to plant and a time to uproot,
> a time to kill and a time to heal, a time to tear down and a time to build,
> a time to weep and a time to laugh, a time to mourn and a time to dance,
> a time to scatter stones and a time to gather them, a time to embrace and a time to refrain,
> a time to search and a time to give up, a time to keep and a time to throw away,
> a time to tear and a time to mend, a time to be silent and a time to speak,
> a time to love and a time to hate, a time for war and a time for peace.
>
> *Ecclesiastes 3:1-8*

The ancient Hebrew sage recognized the cycle of time in life. Not much has really changed in this regard. As we prepare to enter the twenty-first century, we still have not found a magic elixir with the ability to short circuit the healing process. If we want to heal, we must honor nature's schedule. We must take time. Teachers in the Alberta study came to understand this basic need.

> I've got to unburn out. I've got to recuperate. I can't keep running 90 miles an hour and still recuperate. I'm going to need some time to rest.

> I just needed time

> Time. It takes so long . . . You can't rush your body, you can't do anything. You've got to give it time.

> In my mind the primary healer was time away from the situation [3, pp. 54-55].

Taking time just for self-care is very difficult for many caregivers. Not only are we needed to help others, but most of our training programs have prepared us to use every moment productively. It is often difficult to understand that time away from caring for others in order to care for ourselves is "productive" time. Financial constraints have taught us false efficiency. Taking time to rest is just not something we plan to do.

Our Western industrial society has freed up more time for play and recreation than ever before. Yet how often do we swing for an afternoon in a hammock, enjoying the path of the sun across the sky? How many of us will sit quietly in a window seat watching squirrels and lazily reading a juicy novel? Even the ways we play are busy, fast, and challenging. Excitement and competition are the hallmarks of modern "play."

We live in a society of instant gratification. Physicians and therapists are well aware of the wish many people have for a fast and easy cure. Pharmaceutical companies spend millions each year on the search for better, more efficient medications. *Brief therapy* has become the rallying cry of managed care. Students want teachers to provide easy ways to learn, bypassing practice and repetition. Calculators have replaced rapid calculation and slide rules. Politicians cry for more efficient law enforcement. Where burnout is concerned, however, there is no quick cure, no instant remedy.

Time is a gift. Yet when our bodies call us to allow the natural healing which can only happen over time, we usually try to ignore the invitation.

Scott Peck talks about his tendency to assume he cannot perform certain complicated mechanical tasks, when in reality he simply is not willing to allocate the time necessary for understanding their nature.

> But I now know that this is a choice I make, and I am not cursed or genetically affected or otherwise incapacitated or impotent. And I know that I and anyone else who is not mentally defective can solve any problem if we are willing to take the time [4, p. 28].

Most of us have not previously faced personal burnout. We have never needed to take the time to learn to understand the dynamics of this painful syndrome. In fact, many have preferred not to look at this syndrome in the lives of others, in much the same way we often avoid speaking of death.

When burnout becomes a reality, we must take the time to look at it, to understand it in our own lives, and to figure out how to remedy it. Peck tells about the slow process of figuring out how to fix a patient's parking brake.

> I lay down on the floor below the front seat of her car. Then I took the time to make myself comfortable. Once I was comfortable, I then took the time to look at the situation. I looked for several minutes. At first all I saw was a confusing jumble of wires and tubes and rods, whose meaning I did not know. But gradually, in no hurry, I was able to focus my sight on the brake apparatus and trace its course. And then it became clear to me that there was a little latch preventing the brake from being released. I slowly studied this latch until it became clear to me that if I were to push it upward with the tip of my finger it would move easily and release the brake [4, p. 28].

The factors affecting each person's journey into burnout are so intricate and unique that it is vital to take the time to gradually come to understand what went wrong and what we need to do to heal the problem. Peck took the time to look at what seemed an unfathomable maze. Instead of panicking and calling a mechanic, he gave his perceptual system time to orient itself to the situation. Gradually, he was able to sort out all the tubes, wires, and rods and find just what he needed to fix the brake.

A life is easily as complicated as the electrical and mechanical systems of a car. We must allow the time for our perceptual systems to discern what is important and what is not, what is actual, and what is imagined.

Even before sorting things out, we must do what Peck did when he first lay down on the floor of the car. He took time to become comfortable. He knew that unless he allowed his energies to settle and center on the task at hand, he would not be able to figure things out.

In early burnout, we must also allow time for our bodies and spirits to settle into this new and frightening experience. That is what our bodies are telling us by manifesting deep fatigue. Until we pay attention to our need to rest, we will not be able to call into focus other issues which need attention.

When we allow ourselves time for healing, we can rest. Without time, there can be no rest.

RESTING

Tired. I was—all I could do was muster myself to get a coffee and that was about it—get some fresh air. I tried lifting weights. I tried running. I tried swimming but I couldn't—I could swim 40, 50 lengths before, but I couldn't even swim two lengths without getting tired. I put on a lot of weight during that time because I was sleeping a lot [3, p. 54].

You never have any energy, you never have any drive, no get up and go [3, p. 60].

Resting is often very difficult to do. Many caregivers have a strong sense that they must not stop and rest until the needs of everyone else have been met. Robb says that for all professionals, "Setting limits is one of the tensions of professionalism" [2, p. 67]. How much more difficult this is for those professionals upon whom others depend for life quality and safety! For those who have become caregivers because this was a way to live out the expectations of significant others, the burnout experience may be further complicated by a sense of guilt.

> I'm not supposed to get tired or want to rest. I know this. At home, I was the one who could be depended on to look after the kids, to clean the house, and to make excuses when mother was "indisposed." In college, I always handed in every assignment on time. I graduated at the top of my nursing class. I was a unit manager in three years. Everyone in the hospital respects me. Now suddenly, I'm the one needing rest and care. It just doesn't fit with my self-image of myself as the one who helps everyone else.
>
> I'm a fire fighter. Whenever the alarm is sounded, we have a very limited time to get ourselves to whatever emergency is occurring. I can waken from a sound sleep, dress, and be on the truck faster than most people even sit up when their alarm clocks ring. I have trained myself to move quickly and respond to emergencies. Lives have depended on my ability to respond.
>
> Now you're telling me that I need to slow down and relax—good luck! Every cell in my body is resisting. This learning to relax may be the hardest lesson for me.

For some, medications involved in the treatment of physical aspects of burnout may cause drowsiness which, coupled with the endemic fatigue of this syndrome, increases the frustration level.

> The medication—I thought it would help but it didn't seem to help in the way that I wanted it to . . . I couldn't stay awake [3, p. 54].

Fatigue may be a continuing symptom. If it is coupled with chronic pain, the person may experience the double bind of wanting to remediate the pain but needing to hang on to any available energy.

> I know when I was very, very ill, I was in extreme pain. I took nothing for that pain deliberately, because I wasn't going to get myself medicated to the point where I wasn't in control [3, p. 60].

An expert surfer was asked to tell, in a few sentences, what a person would need to know to learn how to ride a wave into shore. He replied, "Put your feet on the board and feel what the waves are saying. Remember that it's the waves that are in control, not you. If you try to fight them and control where you go, you'll lose. You'll go under. But if you feel the waves and their power through the board, if you let go and allow them to do what they can do, you'll end up where you want to go."

This surfing lesson could be thought of as a metaphor for surviving burnout. The experience is so overwhelming that it is impossible for you to take control. But if you will allow the experience to carry you, if you will listen to the experience and recognize its power, eventually you will arrive at the "shore"—the place of healing.

This kind of listening does not mean passivity. Actively listening to the experience, recognizing the power of the waves beneath the surfboard, can be very hard work. Especially if we have lost touch with the voices of our own souls, actively listening may involve clearing away other messages and voices which clutter and obscure what we want to hear.

If you watch a surfer preparing to mount her board, you will see her lie in the deep waves for a while, watching and deciding which wave to choose to ride to shore. In burnout, a multitude of emotions may threaten to overwhelm the individual. A sensation of danger, of potential drowning, may precipitate panic. Like the surfer, we can learn to look at our emotions, deciding which of them are valid, then riding them into shore. We will only be able to do this, however, if we have taken the previous step of settling into the experience and resting until our powers of observation are calm and centered. If we try to short-circuit the process, to skip the first step, we will not be centered enough to begin the effort of real recovery.

Have you ever driven through the mountains, when suddenly your radio music disappeared? You needed to get yourself out of the mountains before you could hear the music again.

Are there mountains which have been obscuring the voice of your soul? What are they? How might you begin to get yourself away from those mountains, to hear more clearly what this experience is saying to you?

For many people, negative attitudes are the mountains which are preventing self-awareness.

NEGATIVE ATTITUDES—
THE STIGMA OF DISABILITY

I always believed that I'd get through this. How, was another thing: how, I wasn't sure. It was kind of like I never ever thought that like, I don't picture myself as disabled, I don't look disabled. I don't feel disabled. I mean I feel I have this stigma about me.

There's a stigma. And I felt the stigma. I came from a family where the work ethic was a very, very important ethic . . . the shame of being on long-term disability—and I've chosen that word shame because I've felt a lot of shame being on long-term disability. And it's something that I don't broadcast around to a lot of people [3, p. 77].

Within most caregivers is a very strong sense of responsibility—sometimes this sense is even overdeveloped. That is often why we don't stop caring for others until we, ourselves, collapse. It is natural then, that we who feel responsible for the needs of other people will have some conscience pangs when we need to stop being caregivers and allow others to care for us.

Many of us grew up in families with the strong work ethic mentioned by the teacher quoted above. This ethic tells us that we *should* be contributing members of society. Conversely, we *should not* require others to be responsible for our needs in any way.

We are aware that people usually imagine that a disabled person would have something about him or herself which looks different—something which shows the disability. When burnout happens, from the outside, most of us look pretty much as we have all along. If there are physical changes, often they happen so slowly that those around us do not notice.

Malcolm was a young man with AIDS. He was unable to eat and permanently in his chest was a feeding tube that was connected to a liquid food supply every few hours. He had another line in his chest through which intravenous medications were administered. All of this was administered at home, with weekly doctor visits. Although Malcolm was extremely thin, when he wore a couple of sweaters, he looked pretty normal. He could not, however, walk very far so when he went shopping, he parked in handicapped spaces. He often had people question him and say things like, "You don't look handicapped to me. Why don't you park where other people do? You're abusing the system!" Malcolm would pull up his sweater and show his chest. Usually that ended the conversation.

Most people who are disabled because of burnout do not have any chest tubes they can show to prove their illness. Many do not want to ask for special treatment. Accepting that words like *disabled* and *handicapped* apply to oneself, even if only temporarily, is often a painful part of the burnout grief process.

Often, the response we feel inside, when we are confronted with this stigma, is a sense of guilt—as if we are not living up to people's expectations. This is often especially so if one is not physically ill. It is much easier, for example, to tell the world that one is resting after surgery or a heart attack, than to admit that one is emotionally depleted.

I didn't want people to see me. I thought, If you're not physically ill, you shouldn't be out. Your parents shouldn't see you. Very guilty.

. . . in a sense I was ashamed, you know, of not being able to cope. You can cope with these things but I can't [3, p. 77].

Often other people give less-than-helpful advice, which can serve to increase the feelings of frustration and shame.

> There are lots of people that think I've been abusive, thinking I shouldn't be taking this amount of time off, that I'm using the system. Might see them on the street, like, You're still off? Isn't it the best thing for you to get back to work? Which was the first thing they ever said. You have too much time on your hands, you should be back to work. Thank you for sharing that with me, but you don't know what you're talking about . . . [3, p. 78].

If this sense of stigmatization is really strong, the individual affected may restrict him or herself from doing some of the activities which could promote healing.

> Last Thursday was the most beautiful spring day, and my wife said, "Let's go for a ride around town and look at the trees in blossom." And I made an excuse because I thought some of the cops who know me might see me and think if I was well enough to play outside, I'm well enough to go to work. I realize that sounds like the thinking of a kid in school, but it's how I think now too.
>
> *a police officer on disability*

> I didn't really feel that it was my right to go and do things. Get out of the house. Have bingo in the afternoon. Do this and that. I gave myself a good talking to one day. I said this is ridiculous. I'm not well enough to go to school. So I might as well have a good time at home. And have kids and grandchildren and friends out to a _____. Just relaxing and getting back to being me again. Looking over my shoulder all the time wondering if the school board was gonna come see what I was up to. Paranoid. It was terrible. I got over that [3, p. 79].

Even the families of disabled persons experience the stigma. Teachers in the Alberta study reported that their friends and spouses seemed less proud of them, and their children invited them less to be with them since their burnout happened. These realities can produce a very lonely and guarded lifestyle which makes emotional and physical healing slower and more difficult. They can even interfere with the person's relationship with his or her personal caregivers. A woman fire fighter shared that when she went to her physician and therapist, "I didn't trust them to believe I was really sick and that this didn't just happen because I'm weak and a woman. Which was especially dumb when you realize that my doctor is a woman. It took a long time before I really trusted that I could tell them how I was feeling."

Anger and a sense of shame and guilt are often complicated by loneliness and a sense of failure. All of these can add up to a loss of self-esteem. Those who have supportive families and friends find that the sense of having people cheering them on is extremely helpful in their ability to believe in and motivate themselves.

> I'm not frightened anymore. I have [relative] in ____ that keeps telling me I am the greatest and he sends me stuff all the time—all this builds you up [3, p. 82].

> My wife's great. Every time we pass an aid car and I sort of cringe and look the other way, she says things like, "It won't be long. You'll be back there again." I know that even if I never work again as a paramedic, she'll be proud of me whatever I do.
>
> *medical emergency specialist*

Even a strong marriage can be stressed by the reality of long-term disability. Already-stressed marriages often end at these times. Some of the teachers in the study, however, related that facing this stressful time actually strengthened their marriages.

> [My wife] was my main support and we were close to splitting up too.

> When . . . you have an extremely shaky relationship it is devastating to realize that you are alone.

> This added stress [spouse on LTD] contributed to the breakdown of my marriage as my partner suffered burnout on my

disease and simply could not provide emotional support any longer [3, pp. 86-87].

It is important that spouses and family members acknowledge the difficulties of their own roles as primary care givers. This is an especially stressful position to be in, watching the painful collapse of a person you love. It is also difficult to know that you cannot save them from the difficult process of self-examination and renewed self-definition which is the healing journey from burnout. Family members walk a fine line between being supportive of, and taking over for, the exhausted one. The fact that tempers are very close to the surface in burnout can make any intimacy very difficult.

> I think to myself, how can this woman that I've been married to for so long, put up with this kind of crap, day in day out.

> She can't depend on me any more. It's almost like losing a husband.

> My husband has been, I'd say, about 95 percent of the time supportive . . . sometimes there are days when he says, you know, this is getting overwhelming. I say, yeah, I know [3, pp. 88-89].

If family caregivers understand that it is normal for even the most loving person to become exhausted and to need a break, they will recognize that it is vitally important that they also look after themselves. It is really sad to learn of a spouse who burns out caring for someone who is burned out. Knowing this helps us understand that the syndrome we call burnout can be a self-replicating monster.

DEPRESSION AND BURNOUT

It is important to understand that while depression is certainly a part of the burnout syndrome, it is a type more closely related to the normal transitional depression of grief, than to what we call *endogenous depression*. While all of the symptoms of clinical depression may be present in burnout, this syndrome will not respond to the same treatments as endogenous depression, which has major internal biochemical and hereditary components. The depression associated with burnout will not be cured until the individual undertakes a major life renewal program. Learning to listen to the voice of one's own spirit, and to speak one's unique life call is a process. The following chapters of this book will encourage and guide you on the journey of discovery which will lead you to cure your depression.

If, however, you have struggled with depression prior to burnout, it is important that you continue whatever treatment program has worked for you in the past and that you involve your medical and psychological caregivers in your burnout recovery process.

Some people do not experience full-scale depression, but struggle for many years with a low-level feeling of sadness. They may have difficulty motivating themselves. They may experience a lot of anxiety. They simply may not be able to enjoy life very much or to ever feel really joyously happy. We call this condition *dysthymia,* and often those who have it never seek treatment because, while they do not really enjoy themselves, they have always been able to cope and get through life. They may struggle for years without seeking treatment.

Dysthymia, like endogenous depression, has biochemical and hereditary components. The stress of burnout can kick a dysthymic condition into full-scale depression. If this happens, medical treatment can be very helpful in restoring the perspective of the hurting person. If you are not sure whether you might fit into this category, ask yourself, "Have I really enjoyed my life? Have I typically had plenty of creative energy? Have I always felt sad a lot? Have I experienced a lot of anxiety?" You might also want to ask a good friend or your spouse for input, because they have observed you for a long time. If you find that your answers to a couple of these questions concern you, ask a professional—a therapist or psychiatrist—for a complete assessment.

If there is a physiological factor limiting your ability to recover from burnout, it is important to diagnose and treat it. Depression can affect you at any time in life—for some it will develop or be exacerbated with the burnout syndrome. For most people, however, the depression associated with burnout is best not treated with medications and needs a more psychosocial treatment approach.

FINDING HOPE

The picture painted by the last two chapters of this book may seem pretty bleak. In reality, although the experience of burnout can be exquisitely painful, many people move through it, finding hope that they, their self-esteem, and their relationships will survive. Where do they find this hope? How does hope work to sustain and motivate burned out persons to walk on through what seems like a dark and forbidding forest?

We have already mentioned the love and support of family, friends, and colleagues. Personal attitudes, while they can point toward shame and low self-esteem, can also direct the spirit toward hopefulness. Where are these hopeful attitudes born?

Some people seem to have a part of themselves which is inevitably hopeful. This *hoping self* sees options when others see dead ends, possibilities when all seems lost. It is of this attribute that the old saying, "When the going gets tough, the tough get going," speaks. Jevne and Zingle say, "It takes various forms—optimism, confidence, trust, perserverence, a sense of being forward moving. In combination, these determine that one will attempt to influence one's situation. . .

> I feel that I'm a worthwhile person. I can still do it. And I accept a challenge of working in my specialty. So I look forward to a moving ahead kind of thing, rather than, say, giving up [3, p. 56].

This attitude is the opposite of the shameful, guilty attitude which hinders healing. Why it is easier for some rather than others to be hopeful derives from a complicated combination of factors. Hope is something we have just begun to study [5]. What we do know is that the availability of emotional support, financial stability, and medical care can certainly free the ill person's spirit to think of possibilities instead of problems.

We will say more about the nurturing and necessity of hope in the next chapter. For now, allow yourself time to reflect on the following questions. Whether you are just entering your professional field or you have bought this book to help you sort out the confusion and pain of burnout, this reflection will support your journey.

REFLECTION

1. Try to remember a time in your life when you felt that you had no options, when life was closing in on you. What was that feeling like for you? How did you cope and get through that time?

2. Look at the following lists. Choose which list best describes the way you feel about your body.

reliable	unreliable
strong	tired
capable	fallible
durable	fragile

   How do you feel about your body, given the words you have chosen to describe it? How do you imagine you would feel if you could choose the other list?

3. Complete this sentence: *Three ways my professional status affects my self-image are.*

4. What aspect(s) of your own behavior did you find in each of the four styles of coping? What does this tell you about yourself?

5. Go back to Tables 1 and 2. Think about your own life attitudes. Do you see "Unuseful Attitudes" which are similar to your own? Where do you think you learned those attitudes? Inside you whose voice is actually speaking those unuseful attitudes?

6. Choose one "Less Than Useful Attitude" you would like to change today. Make a plan to stop this thought whenever it enters your consciousness and replace it with a statement of a "Useful Attitude." If the "Useful Attitudes" in the chart do not resonate with you, think of one which will work and which you can speak in your own voice.

7. Do you ever recognize anger as a feeling within yourself? How do you feel when you are angry? How do you behave? Are you feeling angry about some aspect(s) of your life today? Is it difficult for you to sit with anger and allow it to just be within you?

8. How good are you at resting? What emotions rise in you when you think of a protracted period of resting and simply caring for yourself?

9. Sit for fifteen minutes in a quiet place. Do not read or watch TV. Try not to think. Just become aware of how your body feels. Where are your tired places? Where are you carrying stress? Are you in any sort of pain or discomfort. How difficult is it for you to relax and center yourself within your own physical experience?

10. What are the sources of hopeful support in your life? What do you need to do to emotionally become more aware of these supports?

REFERENCES

1. T. Rusk, *Instead of Therapy; Help Yourself Change and Change the Help You're Getting,* Hay House, Inc., Carson, California, 1991.
2. M. E. Robb, Unpublished Doctoral Dissertation, Department of ED. Psych., Faculty of Education, University of Alberta, 1993.
3. R. F. J. Jevne and H. W. Zingle, *Striving for Health: Living with Broken Dreams,* Alberta School Employee Benefit Plan and University of Alberta, Edmonton, 1992.
4. M. S. Peck, *The Road Less Travelled,* Simon and Schuster, New York, 1978.
5. Participant at The Hope Foundation of Alberta, 11032 89th Ave., Edmonton, Alberta T6G 0Z6, Canada.

CHAPTER 8

Finding a Dream That Works: Courage and Hope in Action

Two roads diverged in a yellow wood,
And sorry I could not travel both
And be one traveler, long I stood
And looked down one as far as I could
To where it bent in the undergrowth.

Then took the other, as just as fair,
And having perhaps the better claim,
Because it was grassy and wanted wear;
Though as for that, the passing there
Had worn them really about the same.

And both that morning equally lay
In leaves no step had trodden black.
Oh, I kept the first for another day!
Yet knowing how way leads on to way,
I doubted if I should ever come back.

I shall be telling this with a sigh
Somewhere ages and ages hence:
Two roads diverged in a woods, and I—
I took the one less traveled by,
And that has made all the difference.

Robert Frost [1]

You are at a moment in your life when the road has taken unexpected turns and led you into confusing—perhaps even frightening—terrain. Ahead lie possibilities you never thought would be part of your life. It may feel as if the choices you make right now carry tremendous importance. When one is experiencing what feels like failure, starting again, following a different life pathway than what one has always expected, can be scary. "What if this path doesn't work out either?" "Will people understand why I need to make these changes?" "Why has my dream not worked, when other people's have? Maybe that means I have some flaw in me, and any dream I have is doomed."

Looking at reality may be very painful and difficult at this time. However, doing so is the only way to begin the process of healing. We encourage you to open yourself to reality, examining your options. We can think of three options: 1) go back to your old job, if it is still available, finding some different way to invest yourself so you will not burn out again. 2) Retire permanently. This may be necessary for those with serious chronic health problems. 3) Redevelop your dream, taking what worked from the old dream and finding new ways to use your talent and skills.

None of these options is easy. Each will take careful discernment and thoughtful application. Having experienced burnout, you are aware of the dangers of proceeding without careful planning. Even so, how does one find the courage and hope to begin again?

It may be helpful to know that just because you have burned out once, you are not more fragile than other people or more likely to burn out again. In fact, having experienced this phenomenon; having taken the time to discern and understand what happened; having reformulated a dream which really is about who you are and what you value, you are probably less at risk than those naive people who think, "That couldn't happen to me." Research has shown that these folks are highly at risk.

Have you ever broken an arm or a leg? If so you are likely aware that when the break heals, that place on the bone is stronger than anywhere else because it has grown extra thick at the point of fracture. Because you are taking the time to heal and making the effort to understand, your psyche will be extra strong. Nobody is impervious to burnout, but very few people understand as well as you what they need to do to prevent it from happening again.

Are you ready to move on? Have you allowed yourself to come to terms with the reality of burnout? Can you allow yourself to grieve for what has not worked? Have you come to a place of peace with the idea that it is healthy to take time just for you?

You deserve your own dream, one which fits who you are, your values, and your gifts. From somewhere deep within you, a voice has been calling, very quietly at first and then louder and louder, beckoning you on a journey toward your authentic life expression. As you become personally centered, you will begin to hear that voice more and more clearly.

Of all the chapters in this book, this is the one which needs slow, reflectful reading. You may read this chapter more than once. Or you may read a section, and then spend some time reflecting or completing an exercise, before moving on. Allow yourself the luxury of time. Remember, for many people, slowing down is step one in preventing or healing burnout.

LIMBO TIME

This is *limbo time*—time without your usual touchstones of professional identity. In this life space, you may feel like an outsider—not really out of the old and not yet into the new.

One of the guys was getting married, and they invited me out to lunch with all the people from our shift. I thought I was ready because I was feeling more energy than a few weeks earlier. But it was really a strange feeling. Everyone was nice and friendly and everything, and some of them asked me when I was coming back. That was hard—to know how to say that I wouldn't be back, even though my heart attack was over. But I could see the old politics being played out, even at lunch in a restaurant. I saw it again, in just a couple of hours. At first, I wished I hadn't gone. But then I decided just to pay attention to what I saw, and I felt glad I wasn't part of that any more. But it would have been much better if I could have told them what I was planning to do next, instead of just giving them what must have seemed like evasive answers.

a fire fighter

This *limbo time* will tax your patience. You may feel as if everything familiar has disappeared. One woman said, "It felt as if I was walking through a misty forest—something from a movie—and none of the trees or stumps was familiar. Often, I felt myself stumble over logs and debris. A few times, I walked through bogs which threatened to pull me down. When I was in that space, it was impossible for me to accept on faith that there was an end to it. It was the deepest feeling of desolation I have ever experienced."

Moving through the burnout experience takes time. There is absolutely no way to short-circuit or circumvent the grief process. It may be helpful for your journey, however, if we add a few milestones to the forest. There are tasks to accomplish along the way and until these tasks have been completed, it is impossible to move out of the forest.

RE-EMBRACING THE OLD DREAM

One of the main grief tasks lies in learning to re-embrace the old dream in a new way. This is similar to the task which is required of the parents of a stillborn child. As they grieve for that baby, naming their little one, and recognizing that they are all united in love and will always be part of each other, they are gradually preparing to reinvest in life's realities without their child. When you experience burnout, it is important to embrace the disappointment of your dead dream, recognizing how far you and the dream traveled together, and how much it will always be part of your life. For although the dream cannot continue to live, it was alive within you for many years. You are who you are today largely because that dream existed. You cannot just slough it off as a snake sloughs of an old, tight skin and finds a new one growing underneath. For the dead dream will cling to you and refuse to be abandoned, until gradually, over time, it allows you to store it within a tender place in your soul. When you can do this, you will be able to respect your pain which comes because the dream could not continue to be part of your life.

Kahlil Gibran's *Prophet* says:

But if in your thoughts you must measure time into seasons, let each season circle all the other seasons,
And let today embrace the past with remembrance and the future with longing [2, p. 69].

This in-between time is the time for making the transition from depending on the old dream, to beginning to build a new one.

Have you ever watched otter families at play? The mother carries her pup on her stomach, stroking the little one as she swims on her back. There is obvious love and joy in the relationship. And when a pup dies, the mother continues to carry it for several days. She still strokes the tiny body, but the joy is no longer there. Finally one day, she allows her dead pup to fall off her belly and it sinks into the water.

Of course, we cannot ask a mother otter about this, but it seems that she understands that her pup is dead long before she lets go of him. She needs a few days in that limbo period—not yet ready to let go of the old and reinvest in the new. And still, after the point at which she lets go, there will be time for recovery, impregnation, and gestation, before she actually has to reinvest in parenting a new pup.

FINDING THE GIFT IN THE PAIN

In the Pacific Northwest where Donna lives, devastating floods are almost a yearly reality. Farmers with low-lying property are flooded over and over again. One woman, gazing over her fields which looked more like lakes said, "This is the hardest time for me. The storm is over, the rains have stopped, and the river has crested. But for now, we can't put any livestock into the fields. We can't plant anything. We can't store or process milk because our buildings are flooded. All we can do is wait. I hate this waiting!"

Asked why they stayed on the farm after multiple floods, she replied quickly, "The flood waters carry nutrients for the soil. Flooded plain fields are some of the most fertile. When the weather is cooperating, this farm is extremely prosperous—because of the floods! That's one of the ironies of farming."

Even in what seems like a natural disaster, there is a gift! The only catch is that the farmer must stand around and wait for the fields to dry and must plant new seeds in faith that the gift will, eventually, become evident. In fact, the nutrients left behind by the flood waters will support an especially fruitful harvest.

During this time, while you may feel like the farmer standing around waiting for the fields to drain, allow yourself to imagine what gifts may be left behind by this experience, and how you might access those gifts to create a more fruitful and fulfilling life.

At the moment, finding a gift in this devastating experience may seem like an impossible task. Don't try too hard. It is important to recognize the power and creativity of your subconscious mind. By far the majority of your cognitive powers are below the level of your consciousness. In your subconscious mind, you are thinking, figuring, dreaming, and planning all the time. Especially when you relax and do not try to control it, your subconscious mind is working out the daily thoughts, experiences, and problems of your life. That is why, after an especially sound sleep, you will often arise with the sudden answer to a puzzling or worrisome life situation. Your subconscious mind worked it out for you.

For now, just tell yourself that one day you will recognize a gift in this agony you are experiencing. Remind yourself that your mind has the ability to make lemonade from lemons. It's fine to acknowledge that right now, you have no idea how this can happen because today you feel completely miserable. Just leave the thought of a better future with your subconscious mind.

LIFE'S BALANCING ACT

For many of us professional caregivers, a huge majority of our self-esteem is tied up in our professional identities. *What we do* becomes *Who we are*. When the ability to function in familiar ways is no longer possible, we may lose not only our sense of personal value, but even our sense of personal reality. A nurse said it this way:

I went back to the hospital today and just walked around some of the hallways. I felt like a ghost. I didn't go to the unit where I had worked, so nobody recognized me. They likely thought I was a visitor for their patients. I became anonymous in this place where my identity had been seated for so long. It was an eerie experience.

A part of me wanted to check the bulletin board in personnel. I could go back and work there again. "Maybe it would be better on a different unit, or a different shift," I said to myself. But my intellect replied, "No, I can't come back to the politics and the frustration."

I need to find out who Norma is. Then I can decide what to do with Norma's talents.

I've been in this (therapist training) program for almost two years, just filling in at parishes on weekends. Last Sunday, I went back to (parish where he formerly worked). People remembered me and were interested to hear what I'd been doing. I was surrounded in the coffee room after Mass. Of course, there were those people who had been the bane of my existence when I was pastor. But this time, I saw them as completely different—as wounded people deserving help. And I saw myself as someone who could give help to people like that. I've learned so much.

Then when I was driving home, questions began to confront me. Who am I now? Am I a priest or a therapist or something in the middle? In fact, can I be both a priest and a therapist at the same time?

It's going to take quite some time, I think, to sort this all out. I also need to find out who I am, aside from priest and therapist. I know I need to discover myself, but these professional hats I wear are so—what?—so enticing—that it's easy just to see myself as "the priest" or "the therapist."

Both these people, a nurse searching for her identity and a priest training to be a therapist, have articulated the need for a balance between who we are and what we do. This task may be at the core of recovery from, and future prevention of, burnout. Allow yourself to sit with the thought, "Even though my dream failed me, that does not mean I am without value. The dream was flawed in some way. But I, myself, am more than the dream. I am a person of many, many facets. The failed dream was only part of who I am, not my whole self. It can be reworked or completely replaced. Because I am a whole person, I have the resources to design a life which fits who I am."

It is only when we understand this balance that we are able to bring who we are to what we do. Only then can we be caring professionals who reach out to others from our own humanity, our real personhood. Only then can we sustain intimate and fulfilling relationships with other people.

> No matter how plain or fancy our teaching methods may be, we tend to teach *ourselves* first, last and always. We will find methods that work for us only as we become clearer and clearer about our own identities, about what is within our integrity to do [3, p. 2].

If our professional identities overpower our private identities, we lose sight of our personal lives. We become deaf to the voices of our families and friends. We eventually alienate those we have loved. We become, indeed, alienated from ourselves.

If, however, our private lives become overpowering, we lose objectivity and professional perspective.

As the priest/therapist above said, our professions are so enticing—the feedback and prestige can be so heady—that it is very often our personal selves which lose out in the unbalance of lives. Yet, ironically, nothing we attempt in life will be fully rewarding if we do not know and honor who we are.

WHO'S IN CONTROL?

Would you consider the idea that one need not invest the majority of one's creative energies into career interests? Do you control your career, or has it been controlling you?

Draw a circle. Imagine that this circle encompasses 100 percent of your weekly energy. Now, divide the circle into sections to represent the percentage of your energy which goes to family, friends, interests or hobbies (play), self-maintenance (rest, personal growth, etc.), and professional work. It seems that there are many areas which need to be considered in life's balancing act!

Now draw another circle and repeat the same exercise. This time, however, plot the sections as you would ideally like your life to be. This may take some reflective thinking so you may want to do it over several days.

What have you learned about yourself and your life habits and values from this exercise?

Now, ask yourself the following questions:

- Do I really need a professional dream? Could I have a fulfilling and creative life without it?
- Is it possible to be a professional but not to give all of myself to that aspect of life?

You do not need to have answers right away. Just allow yourself to entertain the ideas that many very happy, fulfilled people support themselves and their families in non-professional ways, and that many professional caregivers place boundaries around their professional lives so they have enough energy for other life aspects.

BALANCING WORK AND PLAY (see Figure 1)

What do you do for fun? Therapists often find that people who come to them for support do not know how to have fun. Maybe they knew at one time, but have forgotten. Many people grew up in "unfun" environments and have forgotten how to play.

There is another very different attitude from the one described previously. People with this other attitude live to play—they believe that through recreation, they truly re-create their lives in many enjoyable ways. Their professional dream becomes one in which they work in order to support their play.

These people are often competent and caring professionals. In fact, the better they are at their work, the more secure they can be that their work will support their recreational activities.

Is it really necessary to be at one end of the continuum or the other—to eschew playful activities in favor of work, or else to work only so one can play? In reality, most of us fall somewhere in the middle. For many of us, because of the seductive nature of our work, there is a tension in our lives to maintain a balanced

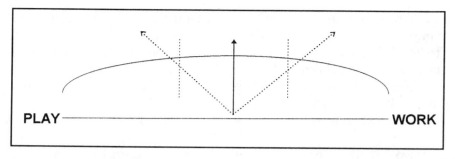

Figure 1. Plot your present position on the continuum. Now plot a position
which feels like it would be a healthy balance for your life. Remember that
you need to look at your average position over time—say six months to a
year—because on any given day or week, you may be heavily over to one
extreme or the other. Balance over a reasonable time span is usually
what works. (The exception is with children, who need
consistent parental attention.)

median position. The more we come to know ourselves, our life
values, and our human needs, and the more we recognize that
we are worthy of respect simply because of who we are, not what
we do, the more easily we can each recognize and maintain our
own correct position for balance.

A group of surgeons meet weekly to work with clay and
glazes in a pottery shop. Their work is supporting their professional art and their art contributes to who they are for their
patients. These people have found a balance between recreation
and work.

Remember, nobody expects you to achieve your perfect
balance immediately. For most people, this is an ongoing growth
experience. It is when we lose awareness of the need to strive for
this balance that many of us get into problems.

UNBALANCED ATTITUDES

Allowing ourselves to work for life balance may mean
giving up some attitudes which are so ingrained within our
psyches that they seem to be absolute truths. Many of these
attitudes we learned when we were very young and in spite of

years of education and experience, we have never questioned them. They are sayings like:

- Any job worth doing is worth doing right
- Work must be complete before playtime begins
- Children play; grown-ups work
- The Devil finds work for idle hands
- Don't begin something you can't complete
- Stop daydreaming and get to work
- Remember the story of *The Grasshopper and The Ant!*
- A winner never quits and a quitter never wins

So strongly have many people been taught these attitudes that they are unable to relax. There are always more tasks—more work—to be completed. Others, who believe they know how to play, have turned recreational activities into attempts at perfection. Stan, a fireman, said "At work, it's vital that we do the job perfectly. One day, I found myself yelling at my ten-year-old daughter, Amanda, because she wasn't the best player on her soccer team. That's the day I realized I needed to loosen up."

Giving up these attitudes may even raise some guilt feelings within us. In fact, by adulthood, many of us have forgotten how to relax. Before we can begin relearning this life skill, we must convince ourselves that we have the right to play, recreate, and just plain relax. How resistant have you been to this concept? Whose voice speaks within you when you plan to play? Where did you learn to feel guilty if you are not always working?

On a piece of paper, write the eight sayings above. Opposite each saying, write an argument which seems more balanced and which makes sense to you. Now, take that piece of paper and place it on your bathroom mirror, to be read and digested three times daily, until you gradually become aware that you are less and less resistant to the idea that your professional career is only one aspect of your life and that there are other equally important aspects.

LEARNING TO DREAM AGAIN

Unfortunately, many adults in Western society have lost touch with their own imaginations. Small children have no problem imagining wonderful places and possibilities. Gradually, however, we learn to differentiate between the real and the illusory. This awareness is a very useful life skill. In our society, however, the line drawn between the real and the imagined is so very absolute that there is no room left for *the possible.* To judge this line, we learned to accept the opinions of those "older and wiser" than ourselves—opinions which often emphasized limitations rather than possibilities.

At very young ages, we were placed into environments where the daily routine was so organized that there was no time left to dream. Certainly, in our school systems, daydreaming is seldom encouraged and often overtly punished.

It is little wonder that, rather than develop our own authentic life dreams, many of us jumped (or were shanghaied) aboard the dreams of significant adults in our lives. There simply were no rewards for dreaming.

Now, however, it is vital that you recapture your innate ability to imagine, for it is only through your imagination that you will open yourself to the possibilities of life. Emily Dickinson said, *"The Possible's slow fuse is lit by the imagination."* In your imagination you can picture yourself in a life dream which is challenging, creative, and fulfilling. As you imagine it, you can come to believe that it is possible to have this life you dream. And there is only a short step between believing in your dream and beginning to make it happen.

> ... one faces a critical choice between "generativity" and "stagnation." Generativity ... is the capacity to turn to the new life that is emerging in the wake of one's own aging ... and to help that new life come into its own. ... Stagnation sets in when those who are aging perceive the new life as holding more threat than promise, and react to the threat by building barriers of self-protection—thereby protecting themselves against the threat but cutting themselves off from the chance for self-renewal as well [3, p. 5].

The first step in relearning to imagine lies in learning to relax. Our imaginations are fueled by the amazing potential of our subconscious minds. When we are involved in the busy activities of daily life, we seldom have time to allow the thoughts of our subconscious to drift to the surface of our consciousness. For this to happen, we must slow down and allow our conscious minds to relax and let go of some control.

Letting go of a portion of the conscious control of our thought processes can feel completely antithetical to everything we have learned since childhood. One man described it this way, "I felt that I was standing at the top of a crevice in a high mountain, and they were asking me to just jump off, not knowing what was down there or how far I would fall, trusting their word that I could fly." It is pretty normal to feel resistant to slowing down and relaxing. Especially when we feel unhappy or uncomfortable, we want to find quick solutions that will help us feel good again. For burnout, however, there is no quick solution, and learning to relax is part of the necessary process. Reflection question number 1 at the end of this chapter is a simple exercise which will help you relax. It can also help you assess how out-of-touch you are from your natural ability to relax.

POSSIBILITIES

Before jumping off that cliff into the unknown crevice, it is important to assess several possibilities. Of course, you may start from scratch, let go of every aspect of your old dream, and move in a completely new direction with your life. There is nothing wrong with that possibility if it feels right for you. In fact, it may feel wonderful to recognize the potential of a completely different lifestyle.

> I never really enjoyed hospital life. The stress of knowing a person's life could depend on what I did in an emergency really got to me. Now I'm looking forward to beginning a new career as a science teacher. I'll still be helping people, but there won't be the high emergency tension and I think my students will be more capable of relating to me than most of the patients I've been seeing.
>
> *respiratory technologist turned teacher*

Ironically, what may be a new and exciting dream for one person may be the life dream from which another is fleeing.

Another possibility is that you may be able to take some aspects of your old dream into the new.

Alice was a nursing nun in an order which ran fifteen large city hospitals. She had risen to a position of organizational prominence within the system. She seldom took vacations, dedicating herself to God's work with the sick.

The year she turned forty-five, Alice began to realize that her energy was greatly diminished from past years. Some days, she had difficulty getting out of bed and going to work. The thought of daily meetings to discuss hospital business became more and more unappealing. Finally one day, Alice walked out of her office at 3:00 P.M. and drove her car to a local hotel. She checked into the hotel and stayed two days before contacting anyone.

The superiors in her congregation were genuinely concerned about Alice and suggested that she spend a few months at a retreat house for nuns in a state where they had no hospitals. They wanted to give her space to think through her future commitments.

In the quiet of the retreat house, Alice began to wonder about the choices she had made in life. Finally, she was sure that she did want to be a nun. She could not imagine herself away from her congregation, which had become her family. Nursing and hospital administration, however, had lost all appeal. In fact, she became physically ill at the thought of returning to her previous work.

A vocational counselor at the retreat house helped Alice understand her interest in people and in helping others. With this awareness, she began to look for options. With her M.A. in nursing, she found that she could train to be a clinical nurse practitioner and open a counseling practice associated with a medical office.

As she began to look into this possible direction for her life, Alice felt her energy and life interest return. Before long, she had registered for the training program. Recently, she joined a practice with two other therapists. She is looking forward to this next stage of her life. She can serve God as a nun and as a therapist.

Alice has been able to take several of the components of her old dream into the new, and to let go of the aspects of her life which were frustrating. You too can discern what you want to keep and what you want to leave behind. Take two sheets of paper and label them *Aspects of My Life I Want to Keep* and *Aspects of My Life I Want to Leave Behind.* Place the two pages on a desk or table where they can stay for several days. Leave a pen nearby. Over a period of time, as you have a thought which would fit on either of these lists, write it down. You will know when the list is complete. Remember, you are simply writing with pen on paper—nothing is carved in stone. You can change your mind or add to the lists in the future as new realizations come to you.

One of the advantages of taking time for rest and centering is that you have more time to reflect upon possibilities. As you reflect, you will come to a point of greater clarity about your preferences amid all the possibilities.

INTEGRATING PERSONAL VALUES

If you reread the story of Alice's discernment process, you will notice that several of the factors which helped her decide among the possibilities were her personal values. Being able to live in her faith community was vitally important, as was her wish to help other people.

Everyone has values, beliefs, and sentiments central to the way you live. For one person, fidelity within marriage might be the highest value, and no career could be considered if it would separate spouses in any way. For another person, the ability to be outdoors and work in natural surroundings might be life giving.

Ben was a teacher. Within a few years of teaching, he realized that the most interesting and creative times he spent with his students were on field trips and overnight camp-outs. As he became less and less excited about his classroom time, he found that he constantly looked forward to those times when he could support his students in finding out about themselves in natural surroundings. He passionately enjoyed those moments.

When Ben saw a job advertised for a counselor/guide with an organization that led teens on wilderness adventures, he jumped at the chance. His career opened up into a new and exciting dimension. He was still working with kids and still teaching.

Only the emphasis was changed, and that change made a terrific difference in Ben's enjoyment of his work.

What values are important to you? Add these values to the list you are making of the aspects of your life you want to keep. Are there values you inherited from someone else but which are not your own, and which have frustrated you as you have been trying to live according to them? Add these to the other list—things you want to leave behind.

DEVELOPING A WHOLE LIFE DREAM

In Chapter 2, we wrote of the many dimensions of a dream. Your new dream needs to take into consideration the many parts of yourself. You are not only a professional person. You are also a person who lives within a social structure. You likely have a family. There may also be organizations or clubs within society which are important to you. What is your world view? Are ecological concerns important or peripheral to the way you want to live? Do you have interests in the world community that need expression in your life? How do you live your spirituality?

Now, as never before, you have a chance to take time to consider these issues. Reflect upon what is and what is not important to you. Begin to discern how you might integrate all the aspects of your life into your dream.

Obviously, if you are drastically changing your life based on your authentic interests, there may be other people whose lives are impacted by your decisions. It is vital that you spend enough time thinking about what you value and why you value those things, so that you can explain these things clearly to those who are important to you. After all, if your decisions impact their lives, they should be entitled to some input on the ways your decisions will be lived out.

Edith, happily married to a well-established lawyer and the mother of two teenage children, found it hard to accept the reality that they were not willing to uproot and move to Kenya, where she hoped to be a missionary teacher. She had come to this desire through fervent prayer and a conviction that God was calling her to those less fortunate than herself. She could not, however, imagine ending her marriage or leaving her children behind.

When they refused to consider her plan, she became deeply depressed. It was a year before she was willing to consider alternative ways or places she might serve God, closer to home. If she had included her family in her discernment process before the final phase, she might have avoided that year of pain for all of them.

It is also very important that you consider timing issues.

Norma was fifty-seven years old when she realized she could no longer function as a teacher. In her youth, teaching was a profession much approved by her parents and teachers as being "suitable" for a refined young lady. Nursing, however, was not acceptable because of "all that blood and gore." All her adult life, Norma had wished she could be a nurse. Now, at fifty-seven, she did not feel emotionally, physically, or financially ready to retire, and she wondered if she could become a nurse. However, looking at the available training programs and the prognosis for the job market, nursing school did not seem a wise choice for a fifty-seven-year-old woman.

So Norma visited her local community college and discovered that it would take far less time to train as a certified nursing assistant. Furthermore, many hospitals were reducing their numbers of registered nurses and hiring more CNAs. Norma entered the program and graduated at the top of her class. Today, she has a very satisfying professional life and is thrilled that she has accomplished her childhood dream.

DEFINING YOUR RESOURCES

Of course, we must always realistically look at factors of funding. Who and what can you count as resources for the birthing of your dream?

Every woman giving birth in a contemporary hospital will have a birthing coach, someone who helps her remain centered, who rubs her back and talks soothingly and even, occasionally, receives the expression of her frustration and anger. (Isn't it interesting that the stage of labor when most women express these emotions is called "transition"? It is usually the time immediately before the birthing happens.)

Is there someone like a birthing coach in your life? If not, can you think of someone you would like to invite to help you in those ways?

What are your own internal resources? How badly do you want to accomplish this new dream? How afraid are you to jump off that crevice of imagination? An old saying goes, "We promise according to our hopes, but perform according to our fears" [4, p. 127].

Being afraid is a perfectly normal human reaction, especially when one has had a huge letdown and disappointment. Even feeling powerless is a normal response to burnout. Fear and bitterness may feel as if they are going to pull you down into a whirlpool. That is certainly a normal human response to disappointment and disillusionment. James W. Moore writes of the choices we can make at times like this.

> . . . when trouble comes, when life tumbles in around us, when disappointment breaks our hearts, when sorrow grips our spirits—*we have a choice: we can grow BITTER, or we can get BETTER!*
>
> I once heard Ralph Sockman express it like this: "A grief is a sorrow we carry in our heart. A grievance is a chip we carry on our shoulder" [5].

Only you can decide how much of your available energy you will continue to give to the past and how much energy you have for this new phase of your life. If you need more time for resting and browsing through life, claim what you need. If you, like the mother otter, need to carry your dead dream a little longer, allow yourself that time. There is absolutely no point to beginning a new leg of the journey until you have been able to withdraw a sufficient supply of your energy resources from the past and invest them in the present. If you allow yourself to honestly process your emotions and energy level, you will know when it is time to take the plunge off that crevice into the vastness of your creative imagination.

Dennis was a fire fighter with twenty-five years of service. One night, in the rush after an alarm sounded, Dennis had a heart attack. He collapsed just before he could climb on the truck. Six months later, he began to accept that he would never fight fires again. Too young to retire, he could not imagine himself in any other profession or job. He often went to the fire station and sat with his former colleagues, drinking coffee and playing cards. Every time an alarm sounded and everyone but Dennis hurried to their response positions, he felt the knife-like pain in his chest again. Dennis told his physician about the recurrent pain. Sadly, the doctor told him that he must stay away from those stressful situations. Dennis became depressed. At that point, his wife insisted that Dennis seek counseling to help him accept his reality.

In counseling, Dennis learned to let go of his self-image as a fire fighter. He began to discover other interesting things about himself. He began working on a new relationship with Laurie, his wife. He allowed himself to consider alternative possibilities for his life.

After two months, he began reading the employment pages of the newspaper. He applied for several jobs which would be less stressful than fire fighting. Nine months after his heart attack, Dennis took a position as a school custodian. It was a very responsible position with the chance to influence children positively. On his day off each week, he volunteered at the same hospital where most of his emergency contacts were from his fire fighting days. Because he understood much of the workings of the Emergency Department, he was allowed to volunteer there. His calm presence in times of crisis, learned from his first career, was a definite asset in that volunteer position and he enjoyed the contact with people.

If, like Dennis, you have been left with permanent disability, be kind to yourself. Everyone has a hard time accepting that they are "disabled" or "handicapped." One thing which may help is learning to "reframe" the present reality of your life. Picture framing shops abound because artists and decorators are aware that the frame one places around a picture can completely change the picture's impact. If you have been seeing your life within a frame labeled "I can't do the things I used to do," then try changing the label to read, "I still have many talents and I can learn new things."

Look at the left side of Figure 2. This figure is about the kind of frame you place around your reality. Your attitudes are the wood from which the frame is carved. An oak picture frame looks quite different from a metal frame. In the same way, when you change the attitude with which you frame your life, often everything looks different. Try to think about the unattractive frames. Are any of them made from an attitude you hold? Do you have any other attitudes that frame your present reality unattractively. If so, write them down. Now, look at the right side of the figure. Here are some possible attitude changes which would create more attractive frames.

Unattractive Frames	More Attractive Frames
• I can't do the things I used to do	• I have talents and I can learn new things.
• If I can't be a teacher (nurse, surgeon, etc.), my life is as good as over.	• I wish that I could still be a teacher (nurse, surgeon, etc.). But realistically, I know that's a bad idea. So I'll look at other possibilities.
• I'm a loser. I can't make things work in my life.	• There are some areas of my life that work. I need to look at what I'm doing that works and realistically assess my assets and talents.
• Everyone thinks I'm a real f _ _ _-up, I can't hold up my head in public.	• There's no shame in honest failure. Lots of very successful people have failures behind them. I need to learn from this experience. Then I'll be stronger than ever.
• I can't face people and say I'm retiring early. They'll think I'm either incompetent or lazy.	• My friends will support my decision. Some people may actually envy me for my excuse to retire.

Figure 2. Framing attitudes.

If none of the more attractive attitudes on the figure seem to fit you, then develop your own. As a picture frame must fit the picture it surrounds, an attitude is only useful if it fits. You may write your own framing attitudes in Figure 2 or use a separate paper.

Accepting the limitations of your body means accepting yourself. It is interesting that many people never really accept themselves as good and worthy until a crisis forces them to be real. It is normal to be sad, to mourn for your health. The mourning helps us prepare to accept what we cannot change and look for alternative ways to live. If you find that retirement is your best or only option, you might look on it as a gift of time to learn and do things you never had time for while you were working.

"That's all very well," you respond. *"But the reason I didn't do all those 'other things' is that my work was important, fun, exciting. Now all I have left are the 'also ran's', the things I never bothered with because they really weren't too interesting."*

Once again, we cite the Serenity Prayer so popular with 12-step program members. Many people facing their own tough realities have been strengthened and comforted by it.

> God, grant me the courage
> to change what can be changed,
> the patience
> to accept what cannot be changed
> and the wisdom
> to know the difference.
>
> *Serenity Prayer*

A TIME TO GIVE BIRTH

I can't believe how afraid I was. All during those months of resting and discerning, all I had wanted to do was get on with my life. Then, when it really was time, I became almost paralyzed with fear. What if it didn't work this time? Would people automatically see me as a loser, when I began again? Was I crazy to think I could start a new career at forty-six? I'd be working with people the same age as my kids! So for a long time, I made excuses. Then one day, I looked around me. It was almost Christmas and my wife was working extra shifts

so we'd have some money for gifts. There were home repairs
we couldn't afford to do. Most important, I was fed up with
not working. I knew it was time to bite the bullet.
nurse transitioning to community college teacher

You have overcome your initial fear of allowing yourself to imagine new and hopeful possibilities. Now, it is time to test some of those possibilities in the real world. Once again, attitude is important. Do you see yourself as a failure, someone whose dream has proven false? Or can you experience yourself as a visionary whose life has had some hard knocks, but who just keeps coming back? You might find comfort in seeing yourself simply as an ordinary person who ran into hard luck, but who deserves and is ready for another chance. Look at yourself in the mirror and think about how you see yourself.

If you find that you are really down on yourself, it may be helpful to read the biographies of some famous people. Most of them have experienced failures and the death of some dreams. But they allowed themselves to re-create their dreams and eventually found the one which would bring success. Donna, in fact, has often been helped by remembering a phrase she heard on the radio many years ago. *An actor must go to approximately one hundred auditions for every good part.* Think of your old dream as an audition. It was one where you had several call-backs. You thought you'd get the part. But that was not to be. Or perhaps you did get the part and the show ran its course and closed. Now, you are looking at other roles. You can't know if this one will be your big break unless you go to that first audition, then the call-backs.

Another attitude that can contribute to fear at this time is shame. It might sound something like, "Everyone knows I've been a failure. This time, I absolutely need to succeed. If I don't, I'll never be able to hold up my head." Or, "I'm ashamed taking a job where I'll be working at the same level with young kids just out of college (or of going back to school, etc.)."

It might be helpful if you could imagine there is a gremlin in your life. This gremlin's name is Paralysis. His job is to sit on your shoulder, whispering reasons why you can't start again. He will use any wile necessary to paralyze you and prevent you from acting positively. He'll tell you to go back to your old, familiar job, even though you know it's bad for you. He'll justify what he says by shaming you. "After all, if you couldn't succeed as a nurse, when millions of other people can, you really don't stand much chance at another profession." Or, "A person your age should be out earning a living, not lollygagging around a university." Your gremlin may have a completely different set of phrases which he knows will work on you. If you can begin to hear what he says, then you have the choice of listening and proving him right (which would make the gremlin happy, but I'm not sure about you) or talking back to him and gradually separating him from your life.

What would be the smallest step you could take today in preparing to give birth to your new dream? Perhaps you could drop by the public library and peruse university catalogues. You might call local employment services—there are often free services run by government agencies or other service agencies such as the YM/YWCA. Does your résumé need some brushing up? There are plenty of books at the library to help with that—or you could invest in a computer program especially written for this purpose.

You do not need to build this towering dream overnight. Take things one step at a time. Recognize that you have some useful skills, but that you may also need to learn more.

LONG-TERM EFFECTS

While most people can reasonably hope to be back at some kind of meaningful life, as a student or professional, within two years, it is important to realize that the scars from something as traumatic as burnout will always be with you. These will likely be lessened with life's successes, especially if the important people in your life are supportive.

REFLECTION

1. Sit comfortably for several minutes with your eyes closed. Breathe gently and slowly—do not change your breathing; just become aware of it. Now allow your mind to listen to

the sounds in the space around you. Concentrate on listening. If thoughts enter your mind, send them gently away, saying that you will pay attention to them later. When you have the urge to open your eyes, resist for a few minutes—spend longer than what at first seems comfortable. Continue to listen to the sounds around you. Then gently open your eyes and become aware of the colors and textures of the space around you. Notice how brilliant the colors seem.

This is a beginning relaxation exercise. For some people it will be very difficult. The level of difficulty you have with this exercise can tell you something about how out-of-touch you are with your natural relaxation ability.

2. Make a list of the five most important people in your personal life. These must not be professional colleagues unless they are also friends. Now imagine asking each of these people for feedback about the creative energy you have been putting into your relationships with them. What do you imagine they would say? Do their imaginary answers give you any ideas for restoring balance to your life?

3. What are some factors you would need to consider in the birthing process of a new dream? Relationship factors? Funding factors? Timing Factors?

4. On a scale of 1 to 10, where 10 is high, how nervous are you about returning to school or doing new work? How do you typically respond to fear? Do you become paralyzed and just become a piece of flotsam, being carried by the waves of life, without any voice about your own preferences or needs? Do you run away and hide (many do this by addictive behaviors)? Do you stand up to the fears and prepare to do battle? It is important to understand our own personal styles because then we can decide whether or not we want to make changes.

5. Spend half an hour in a quiet place, just daydreaming about yourself and the things you would like to do. Allow your imagination to soar—don't worry about reality. Repeat this exercise every day for a week. What themes emerge from your daydreaming? What parts of the huge dream might be suitable to adopt for your realistic life dream?

REFERENCES

1. R. Frost, The Road Not Taken, in *The Oxford Book of American Verse,* Oxford University Press, New York, 1950.
2. K. Gibran, *The Prophet,* Random House, Inc., 1964.
3. P. J. Palmer, *Reflections on a Program for "The Formation of Teachers"*: an occasional paper of the Fetzer Institute, The Fetzer Institute, Kalamazoo, Michigan, 1992.
4. La Rochefoucauld, quoted in *Speakers Sourcebook,* E. Doan (ed.), Zondervan, Grand Rapids, Michigan, 1988.
5. J. W. Moore, *You Can Get Bitter Or Better,* Abingdon Press, Nashville, 1989.

CHAPTER 9

First Things Last–
Burnout Prevention

If the land is living and we are living and our families and communities are living, then *our organizations must be living.* They have souls and unique Spirits that are linked to our culture. *Our organizations can only be as healthy as our culture; and our culture can only be as healthy as our organizations.* As members of organizations, we are called to represent and serve our people—and to care for and nurture the Spirits of our organizations [1, p. 3].

Back in the seventies, there was a move among parents and swim instructors to develop a program to *drownproof* pre-schoolers. It didn't work. Any grandparent could have told them that the developmental stage of a three-year old makes any attempt at or assumption of drownproofing extremely dangerous.

Do we run into similar problems with the dream of creating burnout-proof systems, or even burnout-proof individuals who can handle normal systems? Since the research on which our thesis rests is very fresh, and since such a major task as burnout proofing would take several years at best to develop, we really do not have an answer for this question. It is, however, likely that developmental processes are necessary, both in the ways our society raises and motivates its young and in the organizations within which most adult dreams are planted.

SPIRIT IN THE INDIVIDUAL AND IN THE WORLD

What we would like to do in this closing chapter is dream a bit, look at some very interesting thinking in the professional world, and conjecture about a more hopeful world for those who hurt and those who care for them. The prospect of what this more hopeful world may mean is rather mind-boggling and tremendously exciting. Mike Bell, a management consultant, tells of his reaction to this dawning awareness.

> As you might expect, when all this stuff began to dawn on me, I began going through a vocational crisis. . . . I felt a bit like the prophet Elijah, in the First Book of Kings, who was running from Jezebel and travelling forty days and forty nights until he reached Mount Horeb. He was wacked out and a bit spinney and he went to sleep in a cave. In his sleep he heard a voice telling him to go out and stand at the entrance to the cave because the Lord Yahweh was going to pass by. So he did. And there was a hurricane, but Yahweh wasn't in the hurricane. And an earthquake came by, but Yahweh wasn't in the earthquake. Then came a firestorm, but Yahweh wasn't in the fire. And then he heard, in the words of the King James version, a "still small voice." And it was Yahweh.
>
> For me, as I stood in the mouth of the cave looking out on the organizations I was working with, the answer wasn't in re-engineering, and it wasn't in Total Quality Management, and it wasn't in the self-directed teams or fanatical customer service. It was in the "still small voice" called Spirit [1, p. 6].

Most of us know that sense of deep quiet, that feeling of being right with the world. In your mind, think of driving on a six-lane freeway at four in the afternoon. Just be there for a moment. Observe what happens in your physical body and in the way you feel emotionally. Now, take yourself, in your mind, to the calmest, most beautiful scene you know—the place where you have felt the most right with the world. Notice the differences in both your physical and emotional feelings.

It is not easy to live in a concrete jungle, drive over fifty miles an hour in bumper-to-bumper traffic, and feel *Spirit*. Each of us has times when the clutter and environments of our lives drown out the *still small voice.*

Bell adopts the concept of *Spirit* from the aboriginal peoples of Canada's far north, with whom he has collaborated for many years in the development of their political and economic systems. This Spirit is the manifestation of the unique and special life force or energy within each individual. It corresponds with what we have been calling spirit or the "voice of the soul." Spirit is also in the land, with which the people are in a primary relationship, and in the communities who share the land and interrelate with each other. The communities and the land form the ecosystem.

In the book of Genesis, the ancient Hebrews wrote of the Spirit of Yahweh hovering over the vast, formless void and then beginning to create. God breathed life—God's own Spirit—into the first beings. Creation stories from all around the world tell of this imbuing of life-giving Spirit by the Powers of Holiness, however they are perceived.

THE LOSS OF SPIRIT

In our fast-paced society, often we lose this sense of the sacredness of life and of our ecosystem. Respect for *Spirit* is sacrificed at the altar of *economy* and *efficiency.* Communal links of Spirit are lost in a maze of *individual rights* and *looking out for number one.*

Unfortunately, when "number one" becomes the unit of basic respect, when we stop reaching out to others, our attitudes and actions become self-protective. Our Spirits become small and we enclose them in armor, losing sight of the sacred Spirits of others, of the earth and of community. Isolation and desolation begin to permeate society and hopelessness seeps in. We attempt to ward off the desolation by further tightening our armor. We become more and more discrete and isolated and less and less connected and communal. The tightness of our self-protective armor crushes our Spirits.

Shadel and Thatcher write about what happens at this point. The world becomes a place where we relate to each other as *instruments of commerce*: "a world where my willingness to be civil to you is conditioned on what you can do for me" [2, p. 51].

This is not a new phenomenon. Thousands of years ago, it was written about in the book of Proverbs. "A man's spirit sustains him in sickness, but a crushed spirit who can bear?" [Prov. 18:14].

In contemporary times, psychiatrist Gerald May writes of the human search:

> Our search . . . is a seeking for our deepest roots—not the roots of family, nor of race, nor even of the human species, but roots as creatures of and in this cosmos. It is the sense that, somehow, at some level, we are all One with all creation, and that although there may be some unknown purpose in our separateness, there is also something not quite right with our having forgotten our fundamental togetherness [3, p. 98].

Wouldn't it be wonderful if every child grew up knowing that he or she was a special, unique individual with a unique life mandate, different from the life mandate of any other person, even Dad and Mom, and yet acceptable and lovable, with no need to conform to the interests of others?[1]

Wouldn't it be wonderful if young people growing up could all be inflamed with the excitement of self-discovery so they would build their dreams around their own talents and gifts, instead of around societal expectations?

Wouldn't the world be a more hopeful place if every person was affirmed for his or her own style and beauty? If our schools asked more questions and assumed less answers and encouraged curiosity and tolerance? If collaboration were a skill in which students could "letter" as proudly as they do in competition? If life options were valued, instead of limited and controlled? If the wrinkles in an old person's face were counted as blessings instead of curses and the wisdom in an old person's

---

[1] Of course certain societal controls are necessary—anarchy is not what we are advocating. The line between appropriate societal controls and manipulative control of individuals which prevents personal creativity and violates developmental rights is a fine one. Here, we are speaking of sensitivity to this line.

heart was valued as a social resource? If the concepts *old* and *young* were full of excitement and potential, instead of concepts for devaluing individuals.

If you could dream for a long moment, what would you dream for the world and its inhabitants? What values would you want available for the embracing of future generations? Are these values the values that you live out in your life? How do you do that? Or are there constraints in society—perhaps in your own family—that prevent you from freely living out your values? Are there constraints within yourself which prevent you from living freely the life you would love to embrace?

Where do these constraints come from? What is their power to influence and control our life decisions?

When a baby is born, she has no sense of the other. Her world is centered in herself and her primary caregivers. She attaches to the mother's breast as part of herself and regurgitates on her father's shoulder or falls asleep in his arms in absolute unity and security.

If her caregivers are unconditionally available and supportive, she will gradually move through each developmental stage of recognizing and exploring the *other*, both people and physical environment. For many months, she will hurry back to those people who are part of her safe self-identity whenever her explorations become confusing or frightening. The security of the family will provide a reliable pad from which she will launch herself into life, and this launching will take place over and over again, in wider and wider circles, until she is an adult. The launching pad must be firm enough to push her away, cushy enough for her to run back and land safely, and resilient enough to endure her mistakes and support as she tries again.

In a healthy family, members can be emotionally close, yet each member can have his or her own thoughts, opinions, values, and needs. This ideal is often not the case in reality. In many families, one must choose either closeness or separation.

The problems begin because, for most of us, the nature of the support we receive from childhood caregivers is not one of unconditional love. At a very young age, we begin to learn that nearly everything we try meets with conditional acceptance or even with non-acceptance from the most significant people in our lives. Gradually, as we develop our sense of *otherness* from our caregivers, we develop the sense that we are distinctly separate and not quite acceptable—and perhaps the level of separation is because of our level of unacceptability. We come to understand that if we are going to be loved, it will not be for who we are but for what we do that pleases others. We learn to conform. We put away the imaginations which have so excited and inspired us until now. We set diligently about the task of learning the rules for getting along in the world. At the top of our list of coping priorities is: *get along with parents, teachers, coaches, and any other significant and powerful adult.*

After awhile, our conscious brains become programmed to believe whatever they have been hearing. If I have said, "I want to be a doctor," because my parents have always told me I should, then I come to believe I really do want this. If I have been saying, "I want to be an astronaut, but that is a terrible profession for a girl, so I'll be a teacher instead," eventually, I will believe that I really don't want the hassle of becoming an astronaut.

REDISCOVERING SPIRITS

Beneath our consciousness, however, the voices of our souls, our Spirits, are still trying to speak and be heard, inviting us to become authentic. Part of authentic living, for human beings, lies in the connectedness which manifests the Spirit of community. To be whole, part of what we need is a renewed sense of our unity with all of creation and of the cosmos. Unfortunately, we usually continue to live the internalized restraints we have learned from life, not hearing our soul voices until we become ill. And we develop societal systems which teach and perpetuate in others a continued living of the constraints.

So how can we change such an innate reality of life in our society? How can we help others to become authentic, before they experience the agony of burnout? If we, ourselves, have not reached the point of illness, how can we ensure ourselves to avoid that slippery slope? Since it is unlikely that we will be able to help others avoid a slope we are taking ourselves, we need to answer the second of these questions and then move on to the first.

Hopefully, reading this book and completing the reflections has helped you have a stronger sense of direction in your quest for a balance of self-authenticity with connectedness. Perhaps just settling down into the experience has stilled your life enough so you have been able to hear Spirit's voice within you. Are there further steps you would like to take in getting control over your own life? Perhaps you want to change some habitual behaviors. Perhaps you want to rethink some of your priorities and change to some different pathways for your life journey. Maybe you simply want to continue to live your life with a deeper awareness of your soul's voice, evaluating life along the way. You may have decided to seek professional guidance along the way—medical, psychological, or spiritual direction and support. If you know what you want to do, today is the day to begin the journey anew.

Ask yourself the following questions:

- In reading this book, has my soul voice, my Spirit, been telling me anything important? What?
- Have I discerned anything important about myself? What?
- Do I want to do anything about what I have heard and discerned? What would be the smallest possible step toward making whatever changes I want to make?
- How can I implement that step into my life *today*?

CHOOSING HOPE

For each of us in life, there are *turning points*—moments at which we make a choice toward a positive life change. Sometimes, these moments happen because of important events.

One woman remembers, at age fourteen, sitting beside the bed of a man who was a major part of her childhood, slipping ice cubes into his mouth to ease his dying discomfort. He said, "I hope you live every day of your life so when you go to bed at night, if it were the last day, it would be OK." For that young girl, that moment pointed toward a life of choice.

The mother of a seriously injured young woman said, "There was a day when I knew I had to choose, to either go toward despair, or to turn toward the hope. And I chose the hope."

What is *hopeful* for each of us is deeply personal.[2] We believe the greatest hope lies in living the lives which feel like our own—hearing and responding to what our own souls are saying. When we allow our own hopes to be silenced, we lose the sense of who we are. We lose hope.

People who face a turning point may say, "Yes" or "No" to life. If they choose to embrace life, their "YES" yields more benefit if it is absolute, not, "Yes, if things work out, yes if the boss likes me, yes if my investments go well or my kids turn out."

People who say, "YES" to life understand that "I am more than my family or my job or my mortgage payment. I am ME! I have Spirit! I have a right to listen to the still small voice of my Spirit, and to keep my Spirit as my voice of hope."

Living in hope means acting on hope. *Hope is not about everything turning out alright. It is about life being alright, no matter how things turn out.*

We have a responsibility to embrace life hopefully. For those without a supportive system of family, friends, or colleagues, this will be more difficult. If this is you, your first responsibility may be to look for supportive resources. But remember, nobody else is responsible for enabling you to, or preventing you from, saying "YES" to life. In the end, only you can recognize your own turning points and act on them.

Is this a turning point moment for you? Only you can make that decision. Turning points do not operate like magic. They are inanimate until we give them commitment and life.

BECOMING CHANGE AGENTS

We may never know when our actions or words will lay the foundation for someone else's turning point. Those of us who work with the emotionally wounded know how often we meet

---

[2] To connect with people who explore Hope as an intentional act, who are dedicated to the study and enhancement of hope, contact The Hope Foundation, 11032 89 Ave., Edmonton, Alberta, Canada T6G 0Z6; Phone: (403) 492-1222.

people who have never been told of their own personal beauty, intelligence, or goodness. Just hearing these things may be the turning point in a therapeutic process. Over and over therapy clients have said that the attitude of the therapist— what Rogers called *unconditional positive regard*—was far more influential with them than any spiffy 'therapeutic tool' we pulled out of our bags.

In Dale Wasserman's *Man of La Mancha,* Don Quixote meets Aldonza, a woman who has been rejected by society for so long that she has come to believe society's definition of her.

> I am not your lady!
> I am not any kind of a lady! [4]

Don Quixote, however, saw in her only his own vision of a beautiful lady, his lady he called Dulcinea. He would not accept her self-definition. At first, she fought against his vision of her, telling him that he was the cruelest of all the men who had used her. Her terrible self-image made even the suggestion that she could be a lady too painful to contemplate.

In time, even though the other men in her life decided to put her in her place with a horrible gang rape, and in spite of her awareness that Don Quixote was really the mad Cervantes, Aldonza began to glimpse a hope she had never been allowed to have. For a brief time, one person had seen the beauty in her. At the end of the play, she cradles the dying *Cervantes* in her arms and begs him to remind her of that vision.

> Please,
> Try to remember.
> You looked at me,
> And you called me by another name . . .
> Dulcinea . . . Dulcinea . . . [4]

The amazing thing is that in hearing her new articulation of his lost vision, for one brief and triumphant moment, Don Quixote is restored and *The Impossible Dream* seems momentarily not so impossible.

Don Quixote has usually been interpreted as the story either of a fool, a knight errant, tilter at windmills, or of a hero too hopeful for a jaded society. But *Man of La Mancha* presents this old story as one about relationships, about finding connection where there has only been distance, and of the healing power of unconditional love. Perhaps that part of the story is why it has become a classic, read and loved throughout the generations. It is about all of us, about our need for unconditional love, and for others to trust our hopeful visions of them even when they do not understand. It is about embracing life in a hopeful way.

In meeting others, hopefully, we gradually change society. One woman, who worked with wounded women, said, "Hope is a chain. I am just a link. My job is just to not break the chain . . . and somewhere down the line, they will say, 'I got it!'"

RESPECTING THE OTHER

When we care about others, we often hope they will take the turns we want them to take, embrace the hopes we have for them. Turning points are private. They happen with their own purposes and timing, and they are to be respected. One of the most difficult tasks in supporting the life journeys of others, is often letting go of our visions for them, and inviting them to develop their own life visions

Is there some you know who need you to invite them to share their dreams? Is there someone who needs you to believe in him? Is there someone who has only known negative things about herself, who need to hear your voice hopefully telling her the positive things you see?

Mark, a nurse, was thoroughly disillusioned with himself and with his career. He hated caring for grouchy, sick people. He hated his supervisors at the hospital. He had a difficult time going to work each evening. When he was not at work, he still felt depressed because his work was so unpleasant for him.

Mark decided to enter therapy because he was so unhappy with his life. His therapist suggested three options for him. He could continue in misery. He could change professions, go back to college, and begin a new career. Or he could stay in nursing and try to analyze if there was any way he was contributing to the unpleasantness. If he could figure that out, he might find some ways to change things.

Mark chose the third option and began a journey of self-examination. Over time, he decided that he was definitely alienating those around him at work by his own negativity. He realized that his family of origin had the pattern of never saying anything positive or kind to each other. That was the way he had been relating to others, using biting sarcasm to wound and control. When he knew this about himself, his therapist helped him forgive himself for those he had hurt. Then, Mark decided to change his behaviors. Gradually, he followed an intentional program of behavioral change. To his amazement, just changing his behavior was fun because of the amazed reactions of his friends and colleagues. His patients responded to his kindness with very different behaviors than those whom he had treated curtly or sarcastically.

Mark remembered why he had wanted to be a nurse in the first place. But now, with his compassionate and open manner, he was also a healer.

Turning points can be either positive or negative. What we are inviting you to do is turn away from the outside voices which have prevented you from hearing your own soul's voice, your Spirit.

Ask yourself the following questions:

- What have been some turning points in my life? What was it about those moments that invited me to make changes, to follow a different life course?
- What turn would I need to take to move to a more authentic life, to a dream that could work with me at this time in my life?
- What am I wanting and not acting on? What do I think will happen when I decide to make that turn?
- What do I need to go forward in life? What would I need to leave behind, in order to do this?
- What resources can I use (within myself, others, or society) to support me in making this turn?
- What small thing could I do tomorrow, to contribute to a turning point in someone else's life?

RESILIENCE

Why are some people able to grasp at turning point moments, to bounce back again and again in hope, making huge and productive life changes, while others in similar life situations wander into a seemingly impenetrable forest of despair? Valerie Andrews, in an excellent article in *intuition* magazine [5] discusses the concept of *Resilience*, outlining contemporary research on the subject. This research centers around the stories of individuals who have come up against tremendous negative life experiences and have been able to find the hopeful energy to turn their circumstances around and recreate meaningful and fulfilling lives. One of the basic attitudes which Andrews describes as making the difference is believing, as Buddhism teaches, that "Chaos should be regarded as very good news (because) 'breakdown' is a necessary prelude to 'breakthrough'." People who accept this understanding of life's pain are not surprised when chaos descends, believing this to be a normal life reality. They do not take the pain personally, but set about finding solutions.

Another aspect Andrews cites is the ability to seek out and make use of available nurturing from others. This is an interesting idea because if one accepts it as valid, then the *need to ask for support from others* (something which may bring shame) becomes *the skill to find appropriate support* (something to be proud of). We highly recommend this article.

Resilience and hope go hand-in-hand and cannot be separated. Hope is the sap through the branches of the willow and resilience is the strength of the branches to bend and bounce back beneath the mighty winds of life.

SYSTEMIC CHANGE

As you know, there are two aspects to the dream which must be in congruence to prevent burnout—the personal authenticity factor and the systemic factor. If your dream is authentically your own, can it survive within the system in which you have planted it?

NEW ORGANIZATIONAL PARADIGMS

Mike Bell tells of an emerging group of people who are developing new paradigms for organizational theory because the old paradigms can no longer work in the contemporary reality.

It is hard to tell this story, for it is a story that's just beginning. It's being lived and written about by a precious few people with a consuming interest in organizations who are creating the conceptual paradigm we need to understand organizations in the information age. But, interestingly, they are not seeking answers from other organizational theorists. They need new answers for a new paradigm—so they are turning to the world of cosmology, quantum physics, chemistry, theology, systems theory, psychology—the whole range of sciences and arts. . . .

In this new story, we *always* see organizations in the context of this living universe. We begin to understand that there are forces at work within organizations that we are only beginning to understand—and some of which we will never understand. We live in a world of chaos which every organization needs for its growth—and somehow, mysteriously, order comes out of chaos . . . And in the new scheme of things, information, as Margaret Wheatley tells us, is that spiritual energy force that gives order, prompts growth, and defines what is alive. We are not managing information. Information is managing us [1, p. 7].

For those managers trained by life and education to believe that having control is essential to survival, this approach will be frightening, perhaps even terrifying. For those inspired by the vision articulated by Bell, there is an awareness that trying to develop new theories to fit old paradigms which were not developed for our contemporary reality is tantamount to trying to put new wine in old wineskins.

Neither do men pour new wine into old wineskins. If they do, the skins will burst, the wine will run out and the wineskins will be ruined. No, they pour new wine into new wineskins, and both are preserved [Mat 9:17].

As we become more and more aware that the old paradigms will no longer suffice, yet we are still figuring out the parameters for new paradigms, the time of transition will either be experienced as a void or as a place of exhilarating creativity. Which way will you experience it? The controlling group of managers will attempt to deny the reality, running like mad in attempts to prove the old wineskins still work, sticking their fingers, like the little Dutch boy in the dike, into rips which develop as they look for new theories which the old paradigms can support. The other group will spend much less time running and much more time collectively thinking and supporting each other and creating new paradigms. They may need to spend some money in the process. After all, a new wineskin that will last a long time and serve well may be rather expensive. But oh, how wonderful the payoff of savoring the wine once the wineskin has been prepared, purchased, and filled.

The payoff is not only at the corporate level. Shadel and Thatcher recount the experience of one employee in a company which committed itself to a community-building process "... I now have the courage and the freedom to be myself ... I have learned that being myself is good enough. I accept myself" [2, p. 189].

EVOLUTIONARY CHANGE

Most people resist change. Often this is because we grew up in more or less chaotic families of origin, where getting control, understanding how things worked—was a coping strategy—sometimes even a survival strategy. We learned early on that maintaining the familiar was the safest thing to do. There is a humorous saying, "Just when I got life all figured out, somebody came and changed the rules!" When we read this saying on a plaque, we smile ironically because we can all identify with what it means.

In this case, societal evolution has changed the rules. Just as an agrarian manager (farmer) had to look at a changing reality when the industrial revolution came along, we need to accept the present changing reality. Farmers could not prevent automobiles from taking over the roads, and we as managers approaching the third millennium cannot run away from contemporary developments. In effect, the workplace is at a turning point. Those who recognize the moment will embrace the adventure. Those who don't, won't.

So how can we support ourselves and each other in this time of transition? First, we can give ourselves permission to feel nervous. Psychiatrist Tom Rusk states what he calls the *Familiarity Principle:*

> You cannot act or be treated in ways that are different from those you are used to—even if those ways are better—without becoming increasingly uncomfortable [6, p. 62].

Changes need to be maintained long enough that they become familiar. Then we begin to feel comfortable with them. The *Familiarity Principle* is always in effect at turning points. When we understand this reality, we can usually hang in until the changes become familiar and comfortable.

In this case, the change is a nebulous situation called "transition." How can one become comfortable with something whose definition is constantly changing as we struggle to develop a paradigm? Perhaps, for the moment, we can become comfortable with the state of not knowing the parameters. Perhaps we can hook into the excitement and creativity of building bridges and new structures, and become familiar with "being" in a time of change. Human beings can do this. Even chaos can become familiar. When addicts go into recovery and change their lives from chaos to stability, a major struggle for them and their families is to adjust from the familiar chaos to the new, unfamiliar stability.

It is important to step out into the transition space. It is not really a void. There are others there.

We agree with Mike Bell, who defines the task of management consultants in the 1990s as ". . . spiritual . . . It is helping people in organizations become whole again, by realigning their primary relationships: their jobs to their personal aspirations to their families to their communities, to the universe in which they live" [1, p. 9].

May your Spirits and ours join to create a more joyful and compassionate world. Walk in hope!

REFERENCES

1. M. Bell, *Organizational Development in the Canadian Arctic: The Rediscovery of Spirit,* paper presented to the 1995 Organizational Development Network National Conference, Seattle, Washington, November 16, 1995, Mike Bell, Inukshuk Management Consultants, Yellowknife, Canada.
2. D. Shadel and B. Thatcher, *The Power of Acceptance, Building Meaningful Relationships,* Newcastle Publishing Co., Inc., North Hollywood, California, 1997.
3. G. G. May, *Will and Spirit; A Contemplative Psychology,* Harper and Row, San Francisco, 1982.
4. J. Darion (lyrics) and M. Leigh (music), Aldonza, in *Man of La Mancha,* MCA Records, Inc., Universal City, California, 1973.
5. *Intuition; A Magazine For The Higher Potential of the Mind,* Intuition Network, 369-B 3rd Street, #161, San Rafael, CA, 94901, Issue 17, August 1997.
6. T. Rusk, *Instead of Therapy; Help Yourself Change and Change the Help You're Getting,* Hay House, Carson, California, 1991.

Resources

Ronna F. Jevne, Ph.D.
The Hope Foundation explores Hope as an intentional act. Ronna and the staff are dedicated to the study and enhancement of Hope through interdisciplinary study, workshops, and community projects.
11032 89th Ave.
Edmonton, Alberta
T6G 0Z6, Canada
Phone: (403) 492-1222

Donna Reilly Williams, M.A. is an author, counselor, and consultant. She specialized in support for individuals and groups seeking personal and interpersonal healing and authenticity, through counseling, retreats, workshops, and consultation.
Visit her at http://www.healplace.com on the Internet.
18327 147th Court N.E.
Woodinville, WA 98072
Phone: (425) 402-9027; Fax: (425) 402-6983
E-Mail: donnaRwilliams@juno.com

Mike Bell
Inukshuk Management Consultants provides Organizational Development and staff training services, with a stress on working with the Spirit of the people within the organization—

those closest to the action. Mike and his staff help people bring out the best in themselves, find common ground, and build their own creative future together.
5404 50A Ave.
Yellowknife, NWT
X1A 1G3, Canada
Phone: (403) 873-5042; Fax: (403) 873-9169

Parker J. Palmer, Ph.D. is a writer, teacher, and consultant on issues in education, community, leadership, spirituality, and social change. He can be reached at:
Post Office Box 55063
Madison, WI 53705
Phone: (608) 238-9992

Books by Parker Palmer include:
The Promise of Paradox (Servant Leadership Press, Washington, D.C., 1993)—a collection of essays on community, education, and the inner journey.

To Know As We Are Known (HarperCollins Publishers, San Francisco, 1993)—draws on spiritual tradition to explore the depths of knowing, teaching, and learning.

The Active Life (HarperCollins Publishers, San Francisco, 1990)—an inquiry into the spiritual problems and potentials of work, creativity, and caring.

The Courage to Teach: Exploring the Inner Landscape of a Teacher's Life (Jossey-Bass and Simon and Schuster, 1997)

The Fetzer Institute is a non-profit educational organization that promotes the research and dissemination of lower-cost, scientifically-tested health care methods that utilize the principles of mind-body phenomena. Parker J. Palmer is senior advisor for one of their programs, *The Courage to Teach.*
9292 West KL Ave.
Kalamazoo, MI 49009-9398
Phone: (616) 375-2000; Fax: (616) 372-2163

Annie Whittey
heartfire; the work of respiriting people is a cultural and educational organization directed by Annie Whittey that guides individuals and groups in re-integrating self, community, nature, and spirit. They work with organizations and individuals to restore and care for human nature through seminars/workshops and experiential retreats. Annie's *Plant the Spirit Retreats* offer an opportunity to remember what it is to be in greater harmony with nature, including human nature.
heartfire
P. O. Box 6012
Moraga, CA 94570-6012
Phone/Fax: (510) 376-7231
E-Mail: Anewitte@aol.com

Bay Area OD Network is a professional association of internal and external Organizational Development practitioners in the San Francisco Bay area. *Spirit in the Workplace Resource Guide,* published by BAODN, is a wonderful resource for anyone wanting to discover other individuals, groups, and books about the development of the human spirit in everyday professional life.
BAODN
5 Third Street, 724
San Francisco, CA 94103
Phone: (415) 777-5250

Newsletter: *Spirit at Work*
Judi Neal; Neal and Associates, Management Consulting with sensitivity to the Spirit. Judi is also editor of *Spirit At Work*, a newsletter which should be on the desk of every thoughtful manager. Judi may be contacted and the newsletter may be ordered at:
36 Sylvan Hills Rd.,
East Haven, CT 06513
Phone: (203) 467-9084; Fax: (203) 467-88090
E-Mail: JNeal68321@aol.com

The Foundation For Community Encouragement, through workshops, conferences, and seminars, encourages people in a fragmented world to discover new and better ways of being together. Living, learning, and teaching the principles of community, they serve as a catalyst for compassion, respect, integrity, and authenticity with diversity within groups and organizations. M. Scott Peck is a founding member of this organization.
P.O. Box 17210
Seattle, WA 98107-0910
Phone: (206) 784-9000; Fax: (206) 784-9077
E-Mail: FCOonline@aol.com

For an introduction to the concepts of community building within organizations, as developed and promoted by FCE, read:
Crossroads; "Soul Work" in Organization, by Philip H. Mirvis, *Organization Science*, March/April 1997, Volume 8, Number 2.
Philip H. Mirvis is an organizational researcher and consultant who has been profoundly affected by the work of FCE. He can be contacted at:
P.O. Box 265,
1601 Olney-Sandy Spring Road,
Sandy Spring, MD 20860
Phone/Fax: (301) 774-7377
E-Mail: pmirv@aol.com

For a more in-depth understanding of the profound growth experienced by individuals and organizations who have found the courage to attend FCE workshops and implement community-building principles, and as a gift to yourself as you search for human connection, read:
The Power of Acceptance; Building Meaningful Relationships, by Doug Shadel and Bill Thatcher, Newcastle Publishing Company, Inc., North Hollywood, California, 1997.

Kripalu Center for Yoga and Health is founded on the yogic principles that all humanity belongs to one family and that the divine dwells within each of us. They offer a tremendous variety of individual and group retreat and renewal programs designed to facilitate new levels of vibrant health, peace of mind, and spiritual attunement. Presenting ancient yogic principles in a contemporary, accessible yet profound way, the staff of Kripalu invite you to their *sanctuary for your spirit* in the Berkshires, for day, week-long, and month-long programs.
Box 793
Lenox, MA 01240
Phone: (413) 448-3400; Fax: (413) 448-3384
Web site: http://www.kripalu.org

Institute for Noetic Sciences is a non-profit research, education, and membership organization founded by Apollo 14 astronaut Edgar Mitchell "to expand knowledge of the nature and potentials of the mind and spirit, and to apply that knowledge to advance health for humanity and our planet." They support research and education, develop educational opportunities, and collaborate on critical social issues throughout the world, as well as supporting personal and professional networking. **Visit their web page** at http://www.noetic.org, for a complete idea of their programs and their excellent publications.
475 Gate Five Road, Suite 300
Sausalito, CA 94965
Phone: 1-800-383-1394; Fax: (415) 331-5673

An excellent read, very pragmatic, especially in developing an integrated self-attitude: *The Life We Are Given; A Long-Term Program for Realizing the Potential of Body, Mind, Heart and Soul*, George Leonard and Michael Murphy, G. P. Putnam's Sons, New York. **[This book was published in cooperating with the Institute for Noetic Sciences.]**

The Spirit of Health! publishes an excellent series of brochures in the area of personal and workplace health, healing, stress reduction, and integration. They also publish *Work and*

Spirituality; A Comprehensive Directory To Ielp Managers Improve Performance by Addressing Workers' Spiritual Concerns. This is a great resource.
114 Washington Ave.
Port Richmond, CA 94801
Phone: (888) 224-7685; Fax: (510) 236-1979
E-Mail: khnow@aol.com

Index

About the Authors

Ronna Jevne, Ph.D., holds graduate degrees in Education, Theological Studies, and Counselling Psychology. A professor at the University of Alberta, Ronna has a special interest in the issue of hope and is program director of the Hope Foundation of Alberta, a non-profit group dedicated to the study and enhancement of hope. An international speaker and educator in her field, she is also recognized in Who's Who in Medicine, Foremost Women of the 20th Century, and as the YWCA Woman of Distinction in the Social Science and Education.

Donna Reilly Williams holds a graduate degree in Pastoral Theology and post-Master's credentials in Grief Therapy, Marriage and Family Therapy, and Clinical Hypnotherapy. Listed in Marquis Who's Who in American Women, she is an internationally recognized speaker and teacher and is in private practice in the Seattle area.